59.95

GREAT HOTELS OF THE WORLD: VOL.5

HOTEL RESTAURANT

PHOTOGRAPHY & TEXT
HIRO KISHIKAWA

SUPERVISION
SHINJIRO KIRISHIKI

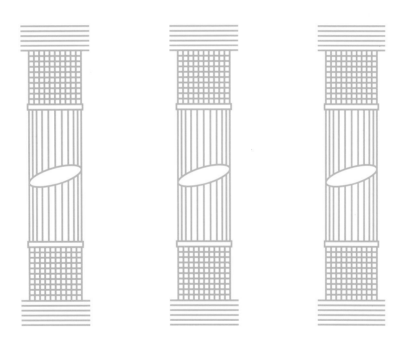

KAWADE SHOBO SHINSHA

序　桐敷真次郎（建築史家・東京家政学院大学教授）

　古代ローマの皇帝・富豪たちの食事メニューが最高に豪華なものであったことから見て、古代地中海地域の旅行者たちが、旅先でパンとチーズと蜂蜜とワインといった庶民の日常食しか食べていなかったとは思えない。古代・中世を通じて、王侯貴族が遠来の客をもてなすのに最善の努力を尽くしたことも疑いない。貴族は大勢の家臣を連れて旅するのが通例であったから、もてなす側も、多数の宿泊室と膨大な量の食事を用意しなければならない。中世後期から19世紀にかけての西欧貴族の館には100室から300室に及ぶ規模のものを見かけるが、客人の宿泊がなければ、これほどの数の部屋を備える必要はあるまい。このような貴族のもてなしが近代高級ホテルのサービスの原型である。

　15世紀の西欧ではイタリアの文化が最高の水準を示していた。メディチ家支配のフィレンツェの富はすべての王侯貴族を凌ぎ、ウルビーノやミラノの宮廷の優雅と壮麗はアルプス以北の支配者たちにとって羨望の的であった。ナイフとフォークのセットがフィレンツェで発明され、15世紀末から16世紀初頭のイタリア戦役を機として、それまで塩をかけた肉を手摑みで食べていた北方の貴族たちに直ちに愛用された。1533年、フィレンツェ出身のカトリーヌ・ド・メディシスがフランス王子（のちのアンリ2世、在位1547-59）の妃となり、オリーヴ油と塩・胡椒主調のイタリア料理を料理人もろともフランス宮廷に持ち込み、それがバターとソースを主調とする近世フランス料理を生み出すもととなった。山海の素材により恵まれたフランスはこうして一躍料理の王国となり、ルイ王朝時代に完成したフランス料理が西欧料理を代表するものとなる。19世紀初頭の大グルメ、ブリア・サヴァラン（1755-1826）の名著『美味礼賛』（1824）はこうしたフランス料理術の勝利の記念碑といえよう。

　しかし、食卓の用具と食事のマナーを今日の姿に完成させたのはイギリス貴族である。17世紀以降、貿易と産業によってヨーロッパ随一の富を築いたイギリスは、西洋最大の海軍国・海運国として、最も多数の海外旅行者を世界に送り出した。彼らは、各国の食事習慣のうち、最も合理的で手落ちのない方法とマナーを取り入れ、それらを最も円滑なシークエンスにつなぎ合わせ、食事の開始前から終了後に至るまで、完全無欠の優雅さをもって給仕し食事するマナーをつくりあげた。すなわち、給仕人が運ぶ金銀の大盆、食物の種類に合わせた何種類も形や大きさのナイフ・フォーク・スプーン、多種多様な皿とグラス、その他、ありとあらゆる食事用具を白布で覆ったテーブルに次から次へと並べ立ててゆく美しくも華やかな食事の方式である。

　イギリス式食卓マナーは、その飽くなき優雅さの追求から、スープを全く音を立てずに吸うとか、フォークの弓なりの背に青豆を乗せ、落とさずに口まで運ぶという高等技術を必要とするものではあったが、その華麗さと上品さで接待用食事の模範となり、結局、味において優るフランス料理をイギリス式マナーで提供することが西欧の宴会、そして現代の国際的食事作法の基本となった。19世紀後期のグランド・ホテルの勃興期にも、世界を最もよく旅したのはイギリス人であり、彼らはイギリス式でないものをあからさまに軽蔑したから、世界各国のホテルのフロントやレストランの作法は急

速にイギリス化されていった。

　フランス料理が西欧を代表するように、東洋を代表しているのが中華料理で、この両者を世界が生んだ二大料理術とみなすことにはほとんど異論があるまい。中華料理の特色は、すべての材料を必ず火に通すこと、犬・猫・蛇・猿・熊・ラクダを含め、どのような素材も必ず調理してしまう魔術的能力にあり、それゆえ最も衛生的で合理的な栄養料理といえる。唐の時代にすでに基本的な山海の素材と調味料がすべて出そろい、宋の時代には山東、江蘇、四川、広東の四大料理の基礎が確立した上、さらに素菜（精進料理）が加わり、清朝に至って今日のいわゆる中華料理十大系統が完成した。そして清朝第6代の乾隆帝（1711-99）が、帝国を巡遊して各地の料理を調査し、揚州人のシェフを北京に連れ帰って創り上げた宮廷料理の極致が、中国全土の料理の粋の集大成「満漢全席」である。これは、最高180種の美味と珍味を二昼夜かけて賞味するという超豪華版で、古代ローマやルイ王朝のフランスにもこれに匹敵するメニューはあったが今は昔の夢、現在、現実に味わえる食事（香港で賞味できる）としては、これが世界最高の料理であろう。世界の二大料理術が、ともに18世紀に完成されたことは特に興味深い。

　ひと昔前まで、超一流のホテルを除いて、ホテルの食事は一般にまずいものとされていた。朝食だけはホテルで摂るが、昼と夜は市中で評判のレストランに行くというのが旅慣れた旅行者の常識であった。しかし、今日では、ホテル側も第一級のレストランをホテル内に備えて、ホテル外のレストランを凌ごうという傾向が目立つ。また、海外旅行が隆盛を極め、地球が小さくなるにつれて、これまでごく一部の人にしか知られていなかった料理が広く好まれるようになるという現象も起こり、各種の珍奇な地方料理を提供する特色ある小レストランをいくつか収容した大ホテルももはや珍しいものではない。

　ホテルの食事は、一般に「ヌーヴェル・クイジーヌ（新料理）」と呼ばれる低カロリー食である。医学知識の普及から、かつては栄養満点とされた高カロリー・高脂肪のフランス料理が健康に悪いといわれるようになり、分量を半減し、動物性脂肪を減らし、しかも味は落とさず、盛り付けを美しくした食事を提供するところが増え、ヴォリュームを誇ったイタリア料理さえ、今やその影響を受けている。上昇中の日本料理の国際的評判も半ばは世界最高の長寿国の健康食としてである。当然、中国精進料理の人気も高まっている。同じ傾向が、菜食主義者や、宗教上の理由から牛肉や豚肉を食べない人々のために特別の食事を用意することを大いに促進している。

　各国にそれぞれ特色ある地方料理が無数にあるように、世界にはまだまだ一般に知られていない珍味佳肴が山とあろう。現代の大ホテルは、こうした新しい特殊料理を発見し、積極的に取り入れてホテルの特色とする余裕と意欲を十分に持っている。それゆえ、世界のホテルの食事は、一方では国際化による均質化も目立つが、大勢として今後ますます多種多様なものとなってゆくであろう。

Introduction by Shinjiro Kirishiki   Architectural Historian and Professor of Tokyo Kasei Gakuin University

The emperors and the wealthy citizens of the ancient Rome enjoyed spectacular meals made up of the finest foods available. Undoubtedly, rich travelers of the ancient Mediterranean also enjoyed excellent food during their journeys, not merely the bread, cheese, honey and wine that were the diet of the commoners. Through the Middle Ages, aristocratic families showed great hospitality to visiting guests from distant lands. Since a noble traveler often brought along large numbers of retainers, the host needed to provide a large number of rooms to house the entourage. From the late Middle Ages to the 19th century, palaces of aristocratic families in Western Europe often contained anywhere from 100 to 300 rooms. This style of aristocratic hospitality served as the model for the services of the modern luxury hotel.

In 15th century Western Europe, Italian culture was supreme. The wealth of the Medici family in Florence surpassed that of all the other sovereigns, and the elegance and grandeur of the courts of Urbino and Milan were envied by the rulers north of the Alps. The use of the knife and fork began in Florence, and during the Italian wars of the late 15th and early 16th centuries, it was quickly adopted by the northern aristocracy, who had previously been eating meat with their hands and daggers.

In 1533 Catherine de Medicis married the French dauphin (who later became King Henry II and reigned from 1547–59), and brought to the French court Italian chefs and dishes, with their characteristic flavors of olive oil, salt and pepper. This was the origin of French cooking, which emphasizes butter and sauces. With the wealth of ingredients from both land and sea at its disposal, French cuisine made great strides, and by the mid-18th century it was at the forefront of Western European cooking. The landmark book *Physiologie du goût* (1824), written by the famous gourmet Brillat-Savarin (1755–1826) stands as a monument to the triumphs of French cooking.

It was the aristocracy of England, though, that gave us our modern table manners and dining implements. From the 17th century England led Western Europe in trade and manufacturing, with the strongest navy and the largest shipping fleet. England also sent the greatest number of travelers out into the world, and as they journeyed from one country to the next they observed the local table manners and customs. Choosing the most appropriate serving methods and manners, the English assembled them harmoniously, creating an elegant serving style which covered every stage of the meal. They used gold and silver platters to be carried by the waiters, knives, forks and spoons, and plates and glasses of various sizes and shapes appropriate for each application. The result was a beautiful, formal table service, with a changing set of tableware laid out on the white linen cloth from one course to the next.

From the insatiable pursuit of elegance exemplified by the English serving style came a corresponding set of table manners—some of them were rather acrobatic, such as sipping soup without making noise, loading green beans onto the back of a fork and transporting them to the mouth without dropping them on the table. The refined manners of the English were combined with the superior French food to create the European-style banquet, which formed the basis for modernday international table etiquette. During the late 19th century, when Grand Hotels were flourishing, the English still traveled the most, and since they showed open disdain for any set of manners which were not English, hotel reception desks and restaurants around the world quickly adapted themselves to the English way of doing things.

While French food stands at the forefront of Western cuisine, Chinese food occupies a similar position in the East, and together they comprise the world's two great cooking styles. In Chinese cooking every sort of ingredient goes into the pan, and a good Chinese chef can work magic with any material, including even dog, cat, snake, monkey, bear or camel, and from the point of view of hygiene and nutritional balance, Chinese cooking has a top reputation. By the time of the T'ang Dynasty, the basic ingredients and seasonings were already in use. During the Sung Dynasty four main cuisines, those of Shantung, Jiangsu, Szechwan and Canton, were established, along with Souchoi (vegetarian) cuisine. The Chinese cooking of the Ch'ing Dynasty was made up of ten major branches. The sixth Ch'ing emperor, Ch'ien-lung-ti (1711–99) traveled through China sampling the cooking of each region, and brought back to Beijing a chef from Yangzhou. There, the chef incorporated the best dishes from each area of the country in special banquets called "All the Best of Manchurian and Chinese Food" which were perhaps the culmination of the court cuisine. With a menu rivaling anything put together for the Roman emperors or French royalty, a typical banquet featured 180 of the finest delicacies of the land and the feasts lasted two days and two nights. It surely ranks as the greatest meals in the world which is still available in Hong Kong today. Interestingly, the world's two great cuisines, Chinese and French, both reached their peak around the same time, in the 18th century.

Up until several years ago hotel food, outside of top-class establishments, was usually fairly bad. Experienced travelers would eat only breakfast at the hotel, but take lunch and dinner at reputed restaurants in town. Nowadays, however, hotel restaurants are gaining in quality and are beginning even to surpass the town restaurants. Also, with the increase in overseas travel, once-obscure cuisines are becoming more popular, and large hotels are opening small, interesting restaurants that offer unusual regional specialties.

Another trend in hotel food is the popularity of low-calorie *nouvelle cuisine*. High-calorie, high-fat French food, once thought to be well balanced nutritionally, is now being blamed for health problems. As a result, restaurants are serving food in smaller, artfully arranged portions, and chefs are producing flavorful dishes cooked with less animal fat. Even Italian food, once famous for its large portions, is following this trend. And perhaps one reason that Japanese cuisine is becoming more popular may be that the Japanese people have the world's longest lifespan. Naturally Chinese vegetarian cuisine is also increasing in popularity, and restaurants are offering more dishes for vegetarians and for people who don't eat pork or beef for religious reasons.

Just as countless regional styles of cooking may exist within a single country, around the world there are still a great many special delicacies that aren't generally known. But as hotels begin to discover these unusual cuisines, many of them are offering them to the public as a means of setting their establishments apart from the competition. So, although on the one hand internationalization can often lead to a greater similarity among hotel restaurants around the world, it can also serve as an impetus for a greater diversity of flavors.

GREAT HOTELS OF THE WORLD: VOL.5
HOTEL RESTAURANT

Photography & Text:
Hiro Kishikawa

Supervision:
Shinjiro Kirishiki

Art Direction:
Toshihiko Kitazawa and Shigeru Morita (Dix-House Inc.)

Translation:
Robb Satterwhite

KAWADE SHOBO SHINSHA, Publishers, Tokyo.
2-32-2, Sendagaya, Shibuya-ku, Tokyo 151, Japan

Copyright © Kawade Shobo Shinsha Publishers Ltd., 1992
Photography and Text copyright © Hiro Kishikawa 1992

All rights reserved:
No part of this publication may be reproduced, stored in a retrieval system, or transmitted, in any form or by any means including electronic, mechanical, photocopying, recording etc., without permission of the copyright holder.

Printed in Japan by DAINIPPON PRINTING CO., LTD.

ISBN4-309-71585-0

CONTENTS

序　　　　　　　　　桐敷真次郎
2 INTRODUCTION by Shinjiro Kirishiki

8 EUROPE
Restaurant Michel Guérard, La Rotonde, Le Café Royal, La Rotonde,
Le Clos Longchamp, Le Paris, Le Prince de Galles, Les Ambassadeurs,
L'Obérisque, Le Cafe Terminus, La Brasserie du Louvre, Les Célébrités, Bell Époque,
Le Louis XV, L'Arlequin, L'Albon Chambon, Grill ABC, El Candelabro, Le Gourmet,
Le Nailhac, Los Naranjos, Salon Azalea, The Pompadour, Selsdon Park Restaurant,
The Dower House Restaurant, Inn of Happiness, Auberge de Provence

60 NORTH AFRICA
Restaurant Le Morocain, Marrakech L'Impériale,
Moroccan Restaurant Al Fassia, Restaurant La Djenina, Citadel Grill,
King Tut Grill, Turkish Coffee Corner, La Mamma

76 AMERICA
Seashell Restaurant, Monarch Room, Midori, Parc Cafe, Kacho,
Silk's, Campton Place Restaurant, The Garden Court, Wellington's, The Beacon,
Checkers Restaurant, Ravel, Hasting's, Gardini, Melrose, The Willard Room,
Bull & Bear, The Barcley Restaurant, Restaurant Maurice, Devereux's,
Windows Restaurant, Palmer's Steak & Seafood House, Cape Cod Room,
Fountain Restaurant, Henry's Restaurant, Windsor Dinning Room,
El Gobernador, Fouquet's de Paris, Azulejos

122 ASIA
One Harbour Road, Grissini, Grand Cafe, Summer Palace, Nadaman,
Tai Pan Restaurant, T'ang Court, Man Wah, Pierrot, Man Ho, J.W.'s Grill, Nicholini's,
Golden Leaf, Gaddi's Lai Ching Heen, The Heritage, Shang Palace, Nadaman,
House of Blossoms, Bologna, Tiki, Hai Tien Lo, Compass Rose, Li-Bai, Normandie

170 AUSTRALIA
The Grange, Horizons, Pericans, Macrossans, Oriental Restaurant,
The Bradshaw Room, Breezes, Kingsfords, Petries, Flinders, The Promenade Café

　　　　　　　　　　　　　　　　谷沢由起子
Esseys (page 8, 60, 76, 122, 170) by Yukiko Tanizawa

●各ホテルの日本での連絡事務所は、キャプション中にアルファベットで表示。
188ページにリストとして記載しています。

EUROPE

ヨーロッパ：貴族の巣から孵化した料理とマナー

　南インドの野蔓からはじけた胡椒の粒は、サハラ砂漠を越えてイスタンブールに着き、さらにヴェニスに渡ったときには黄金と同じ価値を持っていた。時の財閥メディチ家が、その売買権を独占することで巨万の富を築いたことは知られる通り。メディチは一方で芸術家を後援してルネッサンスを起こし、一方で食の追求に情熱を傾けた。そして、カトリーヌが銀のナイフ・フォークと「持参胡椒」を携えてフランスの王室に嫁した時点で、ヨーロッパの社交界にフランス料理が花咲く。

　来賓の貴族は剣をはずして、安全な壁側（上席）に座り、主人は一堂の前で先に酒に口をつけて、毒のないことを証明したあと、胡椒で臭みを消し、味を増した肉や魚の料理をすすめる。淑女の膨らんだスカートのあいだに紳士を配すという、合理的で粋な計らいがなされ、武器とまぎらわしい音や会話を妨げる音は禁じられ……と、貴族の巣から孵化した料理は、マナーとともに今日まで継がれてきた。（谷沢由起子）

Europe: The Aristocratic Origins of Food and Manners

The peppercorns which burst from the wild grasses of southern India were then carried across the Sahara Desert and through Istanbul; by the time they reached Venice they were as expensive as gold. The Medicis, a powerful trading family of that time, used their monopoly on the pepper trade to build a huge fortune. The Medici family were enthusiastic patrons of the arts and one of the forces behind the Renaissance, and they pursued good food just as vigorously. When Catherine married into the French royal family, she brought with her silver knife and fork and a large supply of pepper.

In European fashionable society of the time, French cuisine flourished. Noblemen visiting for dinner would remove their swords and sit in the safest seat in the room, in the far corner against the wall. At the beginning of the meal, the host would take a sip of the wine to show that it wasn't poisoned. Then he would offer meat and fish dishes to which pepper was added in order to mask the bad smell and also to give it flavor. Ladies' billowing skirts took up an enormous amount of room, so men and women were seated in alternating fashion. Plates were laid out and food was served as quietly as possible, so that sounds which could be mistaken for weapons being drawn, as well as noise that would impede conversation, were avoided. In this way, from their roots in the aristocratic practices of the past, food and manners have gone hand and hand, even to this very day. (Yukiko Tanizawa)

MICHEL GUERARD
Les Prés d'Eugénie
40320 Eugénie-les-Bains, Landes. France
Tel: 58.51.19.50 Telex: 540 470
日本事務所：J

1：新フランス料理のなかでも、ヘルシー料理を提供する美食レストラン。鉱泉治療施設を完備したフランス随一のダイエット・ホテル。料理人ミッシェル・ゲラールが精魂こめて作り上げた「子鴨のロースト、青胡椒ソース」と「食通サラダ」。食器はヴィレロイ・アンド・ボッホ焼、グリーン・バスケット・デザイン。2，3：レストランの中央部分。入口に愛嬌のある彫像が飾られている。4：ホテルの中央棟。レストランは1階の左側。5-7：レストラン奥のコーナー。外のテラス部分は宿泊者の朝食レストランとして使われる。

◆◆◆

1: The specialty of this gourmet restaurant is a health-conscious adaptation of Nouvelle Cuisine Française. The hotel is famous as France's foremost diet hotel, complete with mineral spa treatment facilities.
　Among chef Guérard's special dishes are roast duck with green peppercorn sauce (*aiguillettes de caneton au poivre vert*) and a gourmet salad (*salade gourmande*). The Villeroy & Boch servingware features a green basket motif. 2, 3: The central portion of the restaurant. A lovely sculpture stands in the entrance. 4: The central wing of the hotel. The restaurant is to the left, on the first floor. 5–7: A corner of the restaurant. Hotel guests are served breakfast on the outer terrace.

5

6

7

8-10: ホテルのオーナー・シェフ、ミッシェル・ゲラールとクリスチーヌ夫人。ゲラールは1933年生れ。パリのホテル・ド・クリヨン、レストラン・カメリヤを経て、1965年パリ郊外にビストロ「ポト・フー」を開店。料理の斬新さで、世界の食通とパリの有名人が連日連夜おしかけ、結婚記念日に訪れた有名なギャングスターの席がなんとトイレだったこともある。1972年以来、ウージェニー・レ・バンに移り、"おいしく食べて太らない料理"を完成。その功により、1976年度のガイド・ゴーミヨで19.5(20点満点)の最高点。1977年にはミシュラン三つ星を獲得。これらを現在も保持し続けている。1989年、自らのブランド・ワイン「Baron de Bachen」を出荷、ネッスル・フィンダス社から冷凍食品を一般市場へ提供するなど、フランスを代表する料理人の一人である。

8–10: Hotel owner/chef Michel Guérard and his wife Christine. Guérard was born in 1933, and after working at the Hotel de Crillon and Restaurant Camélia in Paris, he opened Bistrot *Le Pot au Feu* in a suburb of Paris in 1965 Celebrities and gourmets gathered from around the world; on one occasion a well-known gangster, visiting the restaurant to celebrate his wedding anniversary, was offered seating in the toilet. In 1972 Guérard moved to Eugénie les Bains and began offering his "delicious, non-fattening cuisine." With its novel cuisine it became known as a gathering place for Paris. In recognition of this achievement. in 1976 Guide Gault Millau awarded his restaurant 19.5 points (out of a possible 20), its highest rating. In 1977 the restaurant was awarded three stars by the Michelin Guide, an honor it has maintained in the years since. Guérard has also introduced his own wine label (Baron de Bachen), in 1989, as well as a line of frozen foods manufactured by Nestlé-Findus. Thanks to these activities he has become one of France's most famous chefs.

LA ROTONDE
Hôtel du Palais
1 Avenue de L'Imperatrice,
64200 Biarritz, France
Tel: (33)59-24-09-40 Fax: (33)59-24-36-84
Telex: 570000
日本事務所：B

1：隣りに位置する美食レストラン「ル・グラン・シエクル（大世紀）」。30席。1-3：皇帝ナポレオン3世が皇后ウージェニーのために建設した離宮がこのホテルのルーツ。半円形のレストラン「ラ・ロトンド」はアンピール様式で飾られ、大西洋を望む。200席。ホテルがあるビアリッツ市はフランス・バスク地域に属し、カンタブリア海からの豊富な魚介類を使ったバスク料理が楽しめる。

●●●

1: Next door is the gourmet restaurant *Le Grand Siècle,* which seats 30. 1–3: This hotel was originally built by Emperor Napoleon III as a summer palace for his wife, the Empress Eugénie. The hotel restaurant, *La Rotonde,* looks out over the Atlantic. Semi-circular in shape, it is decorated in Empire style and has seating for 200 patrons. Biarritz, where the hotel is located, is part of the French Basque region, and the restaurant offers Basque dishes with fresh seafood from the *Mar Cantárico* in northern Spain.

7

6

4,6：「ラ・ロトンド」の食器は、特注アヴィランドのリモージュ焼。5：エグゼクティブ・シェフは、ビアリッツ近郊生れのグレゴワ・セァン。バスク地方特有の低いトク（コック帽）を愛用。ミッシェル・ゲラールのもとで5年、ポール・ボキューズのもとで4年間（うち2年間は東京）修業して現職へ。現在（91年）、ミシュラン一つ星のレストラン。7：ヨーロッパ・アカザエビのバスク風オムレツ、バイヨンヌ・ハム添え。バイヨンヌはスペイン国境に近い南西フランスの町でハムの名産地。8：子豚のグリル・セージ風味、南西フランス特有のガルビュール・スープ。9：秋をイメージしたフルーツとケーキのデザート。

●●●

4, 6: *La Rotonde* uses specially made Limoges servingware by Haviland. 5: Executive Chef Gregoire Sein, a native of the area near Biarritz, wears a Basque toque, a short chef's hat peculiar to the region. Before attaining his present position he apprenticed under Michel Guérard for five years and Paul Bocuse for four years (including two years in Tokyo). At present (1991) the restaurant has one star in the Michelin Guide. 7: A Basque-style prawn omelette with Bayonne ham (*pipérade de langoustines au jambon de Bayonne*). Bayonne, near the Spanish border in southwest France, is famous for its ham. 8: Roast suckling pig with sage, served with *garbure*, a southwestern French stew (*cochon de lait rôti à la sauge, jus de garbure*). 9: An autumn dessert of cake and fruit (*charlotte éclairée de fruits d'automne*).

8

9

Great Hotels of the World: vol. 5 —— 17

LE CAFÉ ROYAL
Royal Club Evian
Rive Sud du Lac de Genève-74500
Evian-Les-Bains, France
Tel: 33-50.75.14.00 Fax: 33-50.75.38.40
Telex: 385759
日本事務所：B

1：レストラン「ル・カフェ・ロワイヤル」には2つのエリアがあり、写真は奥の部分。2：レマン湖を見下す高台に建てられたイギリス王エドワード7世の別邸がこのホテルのルーツ。3：「ロイヤル・ホテル」の名で開業した当時使われていた食器。4：テーブル・セッティング。食器はドイツのフッチェンロイター焼。5：レストラン入口のメニュー。

●●●

1: *Le Café Royal* restaurant is made up of two separate sections; the photo shows a corner area. 2: This hotel stands on a hill overlooking Lake Geneva. It was originally a summer villa for England's King Edward VII. 3: The original servingware bears the former name of the hotel, the "Royal Hotel." 4: A table setting; the servingware is from Hutschenreuther of Germany. 5: A menu posted at the restaurant entrance.

6

7

8

9

6: アボカドと小エビのオードブル。7: ヒラメのブルゴーニュ・ソース、焼きリンゴとシャンピニオン添え。8: チョコレート・ケーキのデザート。9: エグゼクティブ・シェフは中央のミッシェル・レンツ。湖畔の町エヴィアンのミシュラン一つ星（91年）のレストラン「ラ・トク・ロワイヤル」の料理長でもある。

●●●

6: Avocado and shrimp appetizers (*poire d'advocat farcie aux crevettes*). 7: Pan-fried turbot in Burgundy sauce with apples and mushrooms (*escalop de turbot poêlée, sauce Bourguignonne croustillant de pommes aux champignons*). 8: Dessert selections from the pastry chef (*douceurs du pâtissier*). 9: Executive Chef Michel Lentz (center). Chef Lentz is also head chef of *La Toque Royale*, a restaurant in the lakefront town of Evian which has earned one star in the Michelin Guide (1991).

LA ROTONDE
Royal Club Evian
Rive sud du Lac de Genève-74500
Evian-Les-Bains, France
Tel: 33-50.75.14.00 Fax: 33-50.75.38.40
Telex: 385759
日本事務所：B

1: レストラン「ル・カフェ・ロワイヤル」の奥にあるダイエット料理専門の円形レストラン「ラ・ロトンド」地下のボデイ・トリートメント施設と組合わせて利用する宿泊者専用施設。2: 食器はベルナルドのリモージュ焼。絵付けが熱で変質しないデコール・イナルテラブル。1～2週間かけてダイエットするホテルとして世界の富裕階級に知られている。

●●●

1: Specializing in dietetic foods, *La Rotonde* occupies a corner of *Le Café Royal* and is named for the pleated, domeshaped ceiling. 2. The Limoges china by Bernardaud features a *"décor inaltérable"* pattern, which does not deteriorate with heat. The hotel is famous with wealthy patrons from around the world for its 1–2 week diet plan. This plan makes use of both the restaurant and the hotel's underground "body treatment facilities."

1

2

LE CLOS LONGCHAMP
Hotel Meridien Paris
81, boulevard Gouvion-St-Cyr
75017 Paris, France
Tel: 47 58 12 30 Telex: 290952
日本事務所：M

1, 2: パリのメトロ、ポルト・マイヨー駅近くに建つ都市型近代ホテル。中庭に面した一角に、ミシュラン二つ星(91年)を獲得したレストラン「ル・クロ・ロンシャン」がある。隣接するブローニュの森のロンシャン競馬場から名を取り、競走馬を描いた美しいフレスコ画で飾られ、フランス美食料理を提供するレストランとして人気を呼んでいる。

●●●

1, 2: This modern, urban-style hotel is near the Porte Maillot Metro station in Paris. *Le Clos Longchamp* restaurant, which earned two stars from the Michelin Guide (1991), looks out over the courtyard. Named after the *Hippodrome de Longchamp*, a racetrack next to the Bois de Boulogne, the restaurant features a beautiful racehorse fresco on the wall. The establishment has become very popular for its gourmet French cuisine.

LE PARIS
Hotel Lutetia
45, Boulevard Raspail-75006 Paris, France
Tel: 1-45.44.38.10 Fax: 1-45.44.50.50
Telex: 270424
日本事務所：B

1: 1910年パリのサン・ジェルマン・デュ・プレに開業したアール・ヌーボー様式外装のホテル。**2-4**: レストラン「ル・パリ」は、豪華客船の内部を模し、デザイナーのソニア・リキエルがインテリア・コーディネーションを担当。エグゼクティブ・シェフはジャッキー・フレオン。彼は、パリで人気のミシュラン三つ星のレストラン「ジャマン」のオーナー・シェフ、ジョエル・ロビュションが以前エグゼクティブ・シェフを務めていた「レ・セレブリテ」(ホテル・ニッコー・ド・パリ＝P.34参照)のスー・シェフだった。現在(91年)、レストラン「ル・パリ」は、ミシュラン一つ星のレストラン。食器はベルナルドのリモージュ焼。

●●●

1: This Art Nouveau-style hotel opened in Paris's St. German des Prés neighborhood in 1910. **2-4**: Designer Sonia Rykiel coordinated *Le Paris* restaurant, which was fashioned after the interior of a luxury passenger ship. Executive chef Jacky Fréon previously worked at *Les Célébrités* (at Hotel Nikko de Paris-see page 34) as assistant to Joël Robuchon, who is now the owner/chef of Paris's popular Michelin three-stars restaurant *Jamin*. *Le Paris* is currently (1991) ranked with one star by Michelin Guide. The servingware is Limoges china by Bernardaud.

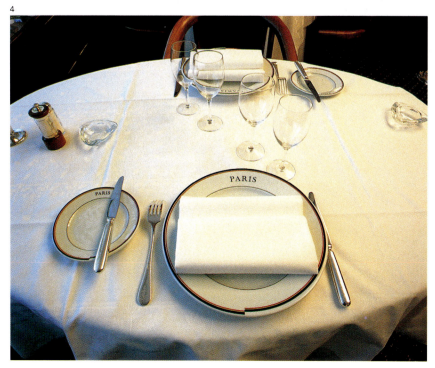

1

2

3

LE PRINCE DE GALLES
Marriott Prince de Galles Hotel
33 Avenue George-V, 75008 Paris, France
Tel: 1-47.23.55.11 Fax: 1-47.20.96.92
Telex: 280 627F
日本事務所：K

1-6：シャンゼリゼ通りから数分という好立地のホテル。ムーア式デザインを取り入れたアール・デコ様式のパティオと室内を持つレストランが「レ・プランス・ド・ガル」。1,5：エグゼクティブ・シェフはピエール・ドミニク・セシロン。食器はベルナルドのリモージュ焼、銀製品はクリストフルが使われている。常時3種類のコース料理が用意され、日曜日にはジャズ演奏付きのブランチ、水曜日の夜にはハープ演奏が楽しめる。

●●●

1–6: This hotel boasts an excellent location just a few minutes from the Champs Elysées. The Art Deco—style patio and interior of *Le Prince de Galles* restaurant are influenced by Moorish design. 1, 5: Pierre Dominique Cécillon is the executive chef. The servingware is Bernardaud Limoges china, and the silverware is by Christofle. Normally a three-course meal is served; on Sundays a jazz brunch is offered and on Wednesday evenings patrons can enjoy harp music while they dine.

4

5

6

1

LES AMBASSADEURS
Hotel de Crillon
10, Place de la Concorde-75008 Paris, France
Tel: 1-42.65.24.24   Fax: 33-1-47.42.72.10
Telex: Reservations-290204 Messages-290241
日本事務所：B

1：メイン・ダイニングの「レ・アンバサドール」は、ミシュラン二つ星（91年）のレストラン。2,3：88年からエグゼクティブ・シェフを勤める南仏モンテュバン生れのクリスチャン・コンスタン（写真：左から2人目）。背後に18世紀の宮殿時代のダイニング・ルーム。4：ホテル・ド・クリヨンはもと国王ルイ15世がパリのコンコルド広場に建てた宮殿であり、現在、重要文化財に指定されている。

●●●

1: The hotel's main dining room, *Les Ambassadeurs*, rated two stars in the 1991 Michelin Guide. 2, 3: Executive chef Christian Constant (second from left) was born in Montauban in southern France, and has been with the restaurant since 1988. Behind where the staff is standing is the original dining room, used in the palace during the 18th century. 4: Hotel de Crillon, at Place de la Concorde in Paris, was originally the palace of French King Louis XV. It is now designated an important cultural property.

2
3

4

5

8

6

5: ホタテ貝にトリュフをはさんだ「サラダ・ソニア・リキエル」。1981〜85年のリノヴェーションでインテリア・コーディネーションを担当したデザイナーにちなんで名付けられた料理。6: いちょうガニのキャベツ包み、オマール・エビの爪添え。7, 8: 季節のフルーツを使ったデザート。食器はソニア・リキエルがデザインしたG.D.A社製のリモージュ焼。

●●●

5: Shredded scallops are a major ingredient of this salad (*fines lamelles de Saint-Jacques en salade "Sonia Rykiel"*) named after Sonia Rykiel, the designer responsible for doing the restaurant's interior during its 1981–85 renovation. 6: Cabbage stuffed with crab and served with lobster claws (*choux farcis aux tourteaux, pince de homard, beurre de caviar*). 7: A seasonal fruit dessert (*délice au fromage blanc, sauce caramel; fruits de saison, pêche Mignonne*). The servingware is Limoges china designed by Sonia Rykiel and manufactured by G.D.A. Company.

7

L'OBELISQUE
Hotel de Crillon
10, Place de la Concorde-75008 Paris, France
Tel: 1-42.65.24.24   Fax: 33-1-47.42.72.10
Telex: Reservations-290204 Messages-290241
日本事務所：B

1,2:「ホテル・ド・クリヨン」の二つ目のレストラン「オベリスク」。同名の「バー・オベリスク」を付帯。以前ここには長いバー・カウンターを設けた「グリル・ルーム・アンド・バー」があったが、1981〜85年のリノヴェーションでソニア・リキエルが改装。ラリックのシャンデリア、バカラのクリスタル・グラス、リキエルがデザインしたリモージュ焼の食器、デコール・イナルテラブルが使われている。

1, 2: The Hotel de Crillon's second restaurant is *L'Obélisque*. Together with the attached *Bar Obélisque*, it occupies the former site of the *Grill Room and Bar*. Designer Sonia Rykiel was responsible for the 1981–85 renovation work. The restaurant features Lalique chandeliers, Baccarat crystal glassware and *décor inaltérable* Limoges china designed by Rykiel.

4

3

LE CAFE TERMINUS
Hotel Concorde Saint-Lazare
108, rue Saint-Lazare, 75008 Paris, France
Tel: 1-40-08-44-44 Fax: 1-42-93-01-20
Telex: 650442F
日本事務所：B

1,2,4：レストラン・ブラスリー「ル・カフェ・テルミニュス」のエグゼクティブ・シェフは、オルレアン生まれのジャルベー・ブロンド。パリ、ブリュッセルのヒルトン・ホテルを経て現職。3：ホテル・コンコルド・サン・ラザール（旧名：グラン・オテル・テルミニュス）は、フランス最初の大型ステーション・ホテル。5：ヒメジのパイ皮包み、オマール・エビのソース。ショーソンと呼ばれる靴形のパイが使われる。6：ツナのリエット。

◦◦◦◦

1, 2, 4: The executive chef of restaurant/brasserie *Le Café Terminus*, Gervais Beaulande, was born in Orléans and previously worked at Hilton Hotels in Paris and Brussels. 3: The Hotel Concorde Saint-Lazare (formerly known as the Grand Hotel Terminus) was France's first train station hotel. 5: Red mullet in a light pastry with lobster sauce (*chausson de rouget, sauce homardine*). The pastry is called *"chausson"* because it has the shape of a slipper. 6: Mackerel rillettes (*rillettes de lisettes à la cuillière*).

5

6

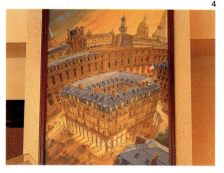

LA BRASSERIE DU LOUVRE
Hotel du Louvre
Place Andre Malraux, 75001 Paris, France
Tel: 1-42-61-56-01 Fax: 1-42-60-02-90
Telex: 220412
日本事務所：B

1,4：1990年のリノヴェーションで改装された「ラ・ブラスリー・デュ・ルーヴル」。2：手前：豚のロースト・ベーコン巻き、編み笠キノコソース。後左：サーモンのテリーヌ。後右：アラスカのクレープと名付けられたデザート。3：パリで最初のグランド・ホテル（近代設備を導入した大型ホテル）がホテル・デュ・ルーヴル。5：エグゼクティブ・シェフのパトリック・サバティエ。6：食器はドイツのショーンワルド焼。

●●●

1, 4 *La Brasserie du Louvre* was refurbished during the 1990 renovation of the hotel. 2: (Front): pork roast with smoked bacon and morel sauce (*mignonettes de filet de porc au lard fumé sauce morilles*); (back left) terrine of salmon spiked with oyster (*terrine de saumon aux huîtres*); (back right) Alaskan crepes, ice cream "Claud" (*les crêpes Alaska, glace vanille chocalat Claud*). 3: The Hotel du Louvre was Paris's first "Grand Hotel." 5: Executive chef Patrick Sabatier. 6: German Schoenwald china is used as servingware.

5

6

LES CELEBRITES
Hotel Nikko de Paris
61 quai de Grenelle, 75015 Paris, France
Tel: 45 75 62 62 Fax: 45.75.42.35
日本事務所：N

1：ミシュラン一つ星（91年）のレストラン。最初のエグゼクティブ・シェフ、ジョエル・ロビュションは、パリで最高の人気を誇るミシュラン三つ星のレストラン「ジャマン」のオーナー・シェフとして名高い。現在のエグゼクティブ・シェフは、「トゥール・ダルジャン」出身のジャッキー・セネシャル。2：パリのセーヌ川沿いに建てられた日本航空直営の近代的なホテルのなかにある。

●●●

1: Joël Robuchon, owner/chef of Paris's most popular restaurant, the Michelin Guide three-stars *Jamin*, was the first executive chef here at *Les Célébrités*. The current executive chef, Jacques Sénéchal, is an alumnus of *Tour d'Argent*. The restaurant boasts an excellent location looking out over the Seine, and it has earned one star in the current (1991) Michelin Guide. 2: This modern hotel on the bank of the Seine River is under the management of Japan Air Lines.

BELL ÉPOQUE
The Hotel Hermitage
Monte-Carlo, B.P.277-MC 98005
Monaco Cedex
Tel: 93.50.67.31 Fax: 93.50.47.12
Telex: 479 432
日本事務所：B

1：モナコ公国のモンテ・カルロに1890年開業したホテル。2-4：レストラン「ベル・エポック」は、グラン・トリアノン（1687年、ルイ14世がヴェルサイユ宮の庭園内に設けた離宮）の内部をイメージしている。デコレーターはアンドレ・ルヴァスール。隣に大サロン「ラ・サル・ベル・エポック」を付帯。食器は特注のリモージュ焼。テーブル上の皿はプレゼンテーション用の食器。

●●●

1: This hotel has served Monte Carlo since 1890. 2-4: The interior of restaurant *Belle Epoque*, decorated in the style of a royal palace, brings to mind *Le Grand Trianon*, the villa French King Louis XIV built in 1687 at Versailles. André Levasseur was the decorator. *La Salle Belle Epoque* is a large salon attached to the restaurant. The servingware is Limoges china. (A service plate is shown.)

LE LOUIS XV
The Hotel de Paris
Place du Casino, B.P.2309-MC 98007
Monaco Cedex
Tel:93.50.80.80 Fax:93.25.59.17
Telex:469 925
日本事務所：B

1-4：モナコ公国モンテ・カルロの由緒あるホテルで、一流ホテルで唯一のミシュラン三つ星(91年)レストラン「ルイ15世」がある。50席。エグゼクティブ・シェフはアラン・デュカス、イタリアン・プロヴァンス料理が提供される。食器は、天井の花柄をモチーフにしたベルナルドの特注リモージュ焼、デコール・イナルテラブル。5：トリュフを贅沢に使った季節の野菜。6：黒オリーブのグラタンを盛ったイトヨリのソテー、新ジャガ添え。

●●●

1-4: This Monte Carlo hotel has a long, distinguished history. Appropriate to its first-class status, it boasts a Michelin three-stars restaurant (1991). *Le Louis XV*, with seating for 50. The executive chef is Alain Ducasse, and his specialty is Italian-Provençal cuisine. The design motif of the specially made *décor inaltérable* Limoges china by Bernardaud echoes the floral pattern of the ceiling. 5: Seasonal vegetables with truffles (*legumes des paysans de Provence mijotés à la truffe noire écrasée, de l'huile d'olive de chez Marveldi, du vieux vinaigre de vin et du gros sel gris*). 6: Sautéed red mullet with new potatoes (*rougets de roche du pays en filets poêlés, un sauté de pommes nouvelles et courgettes à la tapenade*).

Great Hotels of the World: vol.5 — 37

3

4

5

6

7

L'ARLEQUIN
Hotel Metropole-Genève
34, quai General Guisan
CH-1204 Geneve, Switzerland
Tel: (022)21-13-44 Fax: (022)21-13-50
Telex: 421550
日本事務所：B

1, 4：レストランの名「ラルルカン」は、イタリア喜劇の道化役のこと。**2**：エグゼクティブ・シェフは、パリ近郊出身のアラン・ジェニングでミシュラン三つ星の「リュカ・キャルトン」のシェフ、アラン・サンドランスのもとで修業したのち、パリのヒルトン・ホテル、ナイトクラブ・レジーナを経て、8年前に当レストランへ。**3**：ジュネーヴ市のレマン湖畔に建てられたホテル。**5**：鹿肉と魚のテリーヌ。**6**：鹿肉のブリュイワーズ風ソース、梨添え。**7**：フォア・グラとポテトのムースのまわりに大エビを配した、ムール貝とレタスのソース。食器はドイツのフッチェンロイター焼、ジョリー・ターブル。

●●●

1, 4: *L'Arlequin* restaurant is named after the Harlequin of the Comédie Italienne. **2**: Executive chef Alain Jennings was born outside Paris and apprenticed at the three-stars Paris restaurant *Lucas Carton* under Chef Alain Senderens. He also worked at the Paris Hilton Hotel and *Regina* nightclub before coming here eight years ago. **3**: This hotel is on the shores of Lake Geneva, in the city of Geneva. **5**: Terrine of Venison and red mullet (*terrine rouget et sa vinaigrette safranée chevreuil*). **6**: Venison brunoise garnished with pear (*eventail de chevreuil, poires caramelisées, brunoise de céleri au jus de truffes*). **7**: Prawns with mussel and lettuce sauce, served with foie gras and potato mousse (*poêlée de gambas, en rosace, crème de laitue au jus de moules, et son gâteau de pommes de terre au foie gras*).

Servingware is German Hutschenreuther china by Jolie-Table.

1

2

3

4

5

L'ALBON CHAMBON
Hotel Métropole-Brussels
31, place de Brouckere,
B-1000 Brussels, Belguim
Tel:(2)217-23-00 Fax:(2)218-02-20
Telex: 21234
日本事務所：B

1,4：「ラルボン・シャンボン」とは、このホテルを設計した建築家の名。食器はクラシックなローズ・デザインの特注ドイツ製ローゼンタール焼。2：エグゼクティブ・シェフはドミニク・ミシュー。3：ホテル・メトロポール・ブリュッセルは、ブリュッセル市の初期グランド・ホテル。5：アサツキの漉し汁をソースとしたサーモン・ダンス。6：イチゴのミルフイユ。7：軽く燻したタラのフィレ、バター・レモン・ソース、ヨーロッパ・アカザエビと焼きポテト添え。

•••

1, 4: *L'Albon Chambon* restaurant is named after the architect who designed the hotel. The German Rosenthall china incorporates a "Classic Rose" pattern. 2: Executive chef Dominique Michou. 3: Hotel Métropole Brussels was built as one of Brussels's first "Grand Hotels." 5: Salmon in chive sauce (*le saumon dans tous ses états, coulis de ciboulette*). 6: Strawberry mille feuille pastry (*mille-feuille de fruit rouge et son coulis*). 7: Lightly smoked cod fillet in lemon butter sauce with prawns and roast potatoes (*filet de cabillaud légèrement fumé et langoustines aux pommes rôties, beurre citronné*).

6

7

Great Hotels of the World: vol.5 —— 41

GRILL ABC
Ambasciatori Palace Hotel
Via V. Veneto 70, 00187 Rome, Italy
Tel: (06)47493 Fax: (06)4743601
Telex: 610241
日本事務所：B

1：「グリル ア・ビ・チ」は半地下にあるイタリアン・レストランで、シェフはペリッシノット・グイド。北イタリアのウーディネに生れ、カンヌのホテル・マルティネスで修業。ミラノのホテル・パラスを経て、5年前に当レストランのシェフに就任。2：食器は、リチャード・ジノリ焼。3, 6：レストラン・スタッフとレストラン入口。4：ローマのヴェネト通りに建つ半楕円形のホテル。5：手前：蒸しイカとイカ墨ソースのサラダ。左：ズッキーニではさんだホロホロ鳥のロースト。右：ほうれん草入りパスタ。奥：ホームメイドのシシリー風ケーキ。

●●●

1: The chef, Perissinotto Guido, was born in Udine in northern Italy. He apprenticed at the Hotel Martinez in Cannes, then worked at the Hotel Palace in Milan before coming here. 2: The china is from Richard Ginori. 3, 6: The staff and the restaurant entrance. 4: This semi-elliptical hotel stands on the Via Vittorio Veneto in Rome. The Italian restaurant *Grill ABC* is located on the basement mezzanine level. 5: (Front) salad of squid in squid ink sauce (*insalata di seppie al nero*); (left) roast guinea hen and zucchini (*ventaglio di zucchino e faraona*); (right) pasta with spinach and ricotta cheese (*rollatina di ricotta e spinaci*); (rear) Sicilian-style sponge cake with sweet cream cheese, chocolate and crystalized fruit (*cassata alla siciliana*).

5
6

Great Hotels of the World: vol. 5 —— 43

EL CANDELABRO
Avenida Palace
Gran Via Corts Catalanes,
E-08007 Barcelona, Spain
Tel:(03)3019600 Fax:(03)3181234
日本事務所：N

1,2: アベニダ・パラスは、バルセロナ市の中心にあるカタルーニャ広場近くに立つホテル。ホテル建設前の敷地には、豪華絢爛なティー・ルームがあり、当時の優雅な装飾階段が現在もホテル・ロビーに保存されている。レストラン「エル・カンデラブロー」は、カタルーニャ料理の店であるが、魚介料理を中心に幅広い料理が楽しめる。

1, 2: The hotel Avenida Palace is located near the Plaza de Catalunya in central Barcelona. A spectacular tearoom occupied the site before the hotel was built, and an elaborate staircase from the tearoom has been preserved and is now used in te hotel lobby. *El Candelabro* restaurant serves Catalonian cuisine, offering a wide range of dishes and specializing in seafood.

1

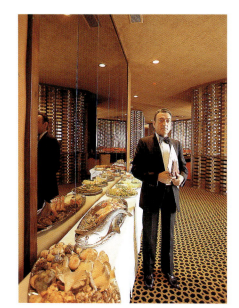

2

LE GOURMET
Hotel Princesa Sofia
Plaza Pio 12, No. 4, E-08028, Barcelona, Spain
Tel: (93)3307111 Telex: 52180 SOFIE
日本事務所：N

1：バルセロナ市の高級住宅地に建てられた19階建の近代ホテルで、開業は1975年。大小9ヵ所の会議室と宴会場を付設するコンヴェンション・ホテルとして知られている。**2-4**：4つあるレストランのひとつが「ル・グルメ」で、内部にプライベート・ダイニング・ルームを付帯。炒めた魚介類をソースで煮込んだ「サルスエラ」、肉と野菜入りの豆シチュー「エスクデヤ」などのカタルーニャ料理が楽しめる。

●●●

1: This modern, 19-story hotel was built in 1975 in one of Barcelona's most fashionable residential districts. Offering nine different meeting and banquet areas, it often serves as a convention hotel. **2-4**: *Le Gourmet*, which includes a private dining room, is one of four restaurants here. It serves Catalonian dishes such as *zarzuela*, a seafood stew, and *escudella*, a stew made from meat, beans and other vegetables.

3

4

Great Hotels of the World: vol. 5 —— 45

LE NAILHAC
Hotel Byblos Andaluz
Mi jas Golf, Mi jas, Apt. 138 Fuengirola,
Malaga, Spain
Tel: 52-473050 Fax: 52-476783 Telex: 79713
日本事務所：B

1： 左：エビとアサリが入ったシーフード・サラダ。右：牛肉のグリル、アスパラガスとニンジン添え。奥：ヴァレンシア風パエリャ。2：スペインのコスタ・デル・ソル（太陽海岸）の街マラガの内陸につくられたアーバン・リゾート・ホテル。3-5：美食料理のレストラン「ルナヤック」は、煉瓦のアーチとタイルで装飾されている。食器は特注アヴィランドのリモージュ焼、デコール・イナルテラブル。6：スー・シェフは、ボルドー生まれのゴンサガ・リシャール。

●●●

1: (Left) seafood salad (*Salade de la mer*); (right) grilled beef with herbs, garnished with asparagus and carrots (*filet de boeuf aux légumes fondants*); (rear) Valencia-style paella (*paella valencienne*). 2: This "urban resort hotel" was built inland from the city of Malaga, on the Spanish Costa del Sol ("Sun Coast"). 3–5: The interior of the gourmet restaurant *Le Nailhac* features brick arches and tilework. The servingware is *décor inaltérable* Limoges porcelain by Haviland. 6: The sous-chef, Gonzaga Richard, was born in the Bordeaux region of France.

LOS NARANJOS
Hotel Don Carlos
Carretera de Cadiz, 29600 Marbella, Spain
Tel:(34) (52)83 11 40
Fax:(34) (52)83 34 29
日本事務所：B

1：コスタ・デル・ソルの街マルベーヤ近郊のリゾート・ホテル。海辺にプール、遊歩道と庭園、スポーツ施設を配し、内陸側にホテル棟がある。2-5：レストラン「ロス・ナランホス(オレンジの園)」では、アンダルシア料理が楽しめる。食器はスイス製のランゼンタール焼。冷たいスープの「ガスパチョ」、ガーリック・スープの「アホ・ブランコ」、「ペスカード・フリト」と呼ばれる魚のフライがおすすめ料理。

1: This resort hotel is located on the outskirts of the town of Marbella on Spain's Costa del Sol. A swimming pool, promenade, garden and various sports facilities face the sea, while the guest room wing is built on the inland side. 2–5: *Los Naranjos* ("The Oranges") serves Andalusian cuisine, including such dishes as *gaspacho* (cold vegetable soup), *ajo blanco* (garlic soup) and *pescado frito* (fried fish). The servingware is Swiss Langenthal china.

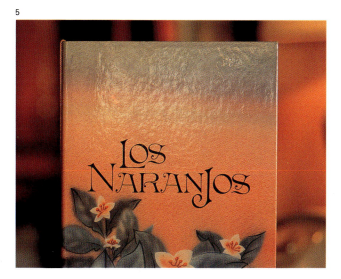

SALON AZALEA
Hotel Plaza
Plaza de España, Madrid 28013, Spain
Tel:(1)247 1200 Fax:(1)248 2389
日本事務所：N

1： 天井を寄木細工で飾ったレストラン「サロン・アサレア」は、昼食ビュッフェを提供するが、レストラン・バーも付設。2： 朝食専用のレストラン「サロン・トレド」。写真は朝食用のビュッフェ・テーブル。スペインならではの多種多様なハムが楽しめる。3： ドン・キホーテとサンチョ・パンサの銅像のあるマドリッドのスペイン広場に面するホテル。

●●●

1: *Salon Azalea* has an ornately crafted ceiling. The restaurant serves a luncheon buffet and also has a bar. 2: *Salon Toledo* serves only breakfast. The breakfast buffet table is shown. One particularly Spanish feature is the wide variety of different types of ham. 3: This Madrid hotel faces the Plaza de España, known for its statues of Don Quijote and Sancho Panza.

POMPADOUR
Caledonian Hotel
Princes Street, Edinburgh EH1 2AB
Scotland, G, Britain
Tel: 031-225-2433 Fax: 031-225-6632
Telex: 72179
日本事務所：I

1： カレドニアン鉄道のステーション・ホテルとして開発されたスコットランドの古都エディンバラのホテル。2,3： 岩山に立つエディンバラ城を眺望するレストラン「ザ・ポンパドール」。専用のレストラン・バーを付帯し、珍しい伝説的なスコットランド料理が楽しめる。テーブル上の料理は左から、ヒラメのグリル、貽貝のパテ、サーモンを円形に巻いたポーチ、奥が牛フィレのグリル。

1: This hotel, in the Scottish capital of Edinburgh, was originally built as a station hotel at the terminus of the Caledonian Railway. 2, 3: *The Pompadour* restaurant looks out over Edinburgh Castle, built on a rugged cliff. The restaurant includes a bar, and it serves legendary Scottish cuisine. (From left) grilled turbot; mussel and onion paté; poached salmon steak with leek sabayon; Aberdeenshire grilled fillet of beef.

SELSDON PARK RESTAURANT
Selsdon Park Hotel
Sanderstead, South Croydon,
Surrey, CR2 8YA, G, Britain
Tel:(081)657-8811 Fax:(081)651-6171
Telex:945003
日本事務所：B

1：エグゼクティブ・シェフはフレディー・ジョーンズ。ロンドンのサヴォイ・ホテルでの皿洗いからスタートしたベテラン。現在では、別の地にグルメ・レストランも所有している。料理は前列左より：牛フィレ・ステーキ・セルスドン風、スモーク・サーモン、仔ヒツジのコヴェント・ガーデン風。後列左から：雌牛のレバーと仔牛のソーセージ、鮮魚のメドレー。2：ロンドン南方21kmのお屋敷ホテルで、18ホールのゴルフ・コースを付設。3：昼食のオードヴルのセッティング。4：レストラン内部の出窓のコーナー。5：テーブル・セッティング。

1: Freddie Jones, the executive chef, had his first job at The Savoy, Hotel in London, where he was a dishwasher for six weeks. He also owns his own gourmet restaurant, at a separate location. (Front row from left) fillet of beef Selsdon; rosette of smoked salmon; lamb Covent Garden style. (Back row from left) calf's liver with veal sausages; medley of fresh fish. 2: This mansion-style hotel is 21 kilometers south of London, and it includes an 18-hole golf course. 3-5: Luncheon hors d'oeuvres; an interior window corner; a table setting.

4

5

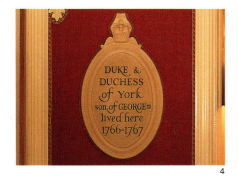

THE DOWER HOUSE RESTAURANT
The Royal Crescent Hotel
16 Royal Crescent, Bath,
Avon BA1 2LS, G, Britain
Tel:0225-319-090 Fax:0225-339401
Telex:444251
日本事務所：1

1,6：レストランは窓側と中央部に分けられ、「ダウワー・ハウス」を描いたプレゼンテーション用食器を使い、イギリス風にアレンジしたフランス料理が提供される。2：イギリスの温泉保養地バースの歴史的建造物ロイヤル・クレッセントの一角に設けられたホテル。3,7：入口に同名の「バー」と「ラウンジ」がある。 4：18世紀の国王ジョージ3世の第2王子ヨーク公が、この建物の一部を別邸として借用していた。5：裏庭の別棟「ザ・ダウワー・ハウス」1階にある「ザ・ダウワー・ハウス・レストラン」。

●●●

1, 6: The restaurant is divided into a window side section and a central area. The service plates are inscribed with the name "The Dower House." The specialty is French cuisine, arranged in an English style. 2: This hotel occupies part of the historical Royal Crescent, Bath famous health resort with thermal springs in England. 3, 7: A bar and lounge are at the entrance to the restaurant. 4: In the late 18th century Frederick Augustus, Duke of York (the second son of King George III) borrowed part of The Royal Crescent Hotel for use as a summer villa. 5: *The Dower House Restaurant* occupies the first floor of *The Dower House*, a separate wing located in the rear garden.

2

INN OF HAPPINESS
St. James Court
Buckingham Gate,
London SW1E 6AF, G, Britain
Tel:01-834-6655 Fax:01-630-7587
Telex:938075 TAJJAM G
日本事務所：B

1：レストラン「イン・オブ・ハッピネス」は、ロンドンでも指折りの中華レストランとして著名。2：セント・ジェームズ・コートは、バッキンガム宮殿に隣接している。3：スタッフ。左から：アラン・チェウ（アシスタント・レストラン・マネージャー）、ミッシェル・ファン（シェフ）、フランキー・ロ（マネージャー）。料理は左から：四川風キング・プローン、北京ダック、醤油と生姜などで味付けしたスズキの姿蒸し。4：中国王朝時代の人物をデザインしたメニュー。

●●●

1: The *Inn of Happiness* is one of London's prominent Chinese restaurants. 2: St. James Court Hotel is near Buckingham Palace. 3: Staff (from left): Alan Cheung (assistant restaurant manager); Michael Fung (chef); Frankie Lok (manager). Dishes (from left): Szechwan-style king prawns; Peking duck; whole sea bass steamed with soy sauce, ginger and spring onions. 4: The menu design incorporates Chinese dynasty-era figures.

3

4

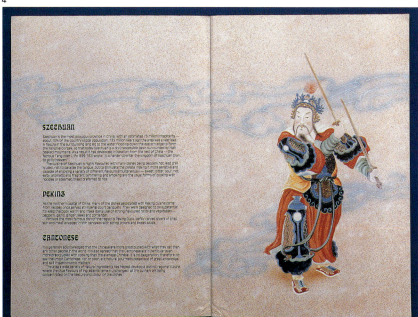

Great Hotels of the World: vol. 5 —— 57

1
2

4

3

AUBERGE DE PROVENCE
St. James Court
Buckingham Gate,
London SW1E 6AF, G, Britain
Tel: 01-834-6655 Fax: 01-630-7587
Telex: 938075 TAJJAM G
日本事務所：B

1：食器はベルナルドのリモージュ焼。食器と同じ柄のナプキンは、レストラン「ウストー・ド・ボーマニエール」のオーナーだったレイモン・テュイリエーが自らデザインした。2：写真左から、レストラン・マネージャーのジル・ペロダンとソムリエのイヴ・ソブァ。3-6：「オーベルジュ・ド・プロヴァンス」はホテルのメイン・ダイニングで、南仏プロヴァンス地方のミシュラン三つ星（90年）のレストラン「ウストー・ド・ボーマニエール」の料理を受け継ぐ美食レストラン。

●●●

1: The servingware and matching napkins were designed by Raymond Thuilier, the owner of *Oustaù de Baumanière*. The servingware is Limoges china by Bernardaud. 2: (From left) Restaurant manager Gilles Perraudin and sommelier Yves Sauboua. 3-6: *Auberge de Provence* serves as the hotel's main dining room. The cooking style and recipes follow those of the three-stars Michelin-rated restaurant (1990) *Oustaù de Baumanière* in the Provence region of southern France.

5

6

NORTH AFRICA

中東(北アフリカ)：幻想の食卓

　美しいシェーラザードが語る「アラビアン・ナイト」の世界は、いまもイスラム式饗宴によみがえる。大理石の床に敷かれた絹のじゅうたん。主賓はラー（太陽神）にちなんで東に座をとり、あとは円陣にすわる。中央に銀の大盆が置かれる。羊の白い脳ミソがうやうやしく運びこまれ、主賓から手をつける。そう、軽い豆腐といった感じ。次に、クスクス――地中海沿岸、とくに北アフリカ共通の煮込み料理。肉や野菜を金串に刺して焼いたケバブ。薄いパン。陶器の壺に入ったタジン・シチューの横には、香草に飾られたハトが眠っている。グリーンのスープは、モロヘアか。香り高いコーヒーか、ミントティーでフィナーレ。

　手で食べる。招いた家のあるじ自ら客の皿に配ることもある。ときどき水で手を洗う。ガラス器に浮かぶバラの花びら。もともと、ローズ・ウォーターは遠来の客をねぎらうアラブの風習だった。虹色の衣装で踊る少女たち。…やがて夜明けを告げるコーランの声。

（谷沢由起子）

The Islamic World: A Table of Fantasy

To take part in an Islamic-style feast, even today, is to return to the world of the Arabian Nights of Scheherazade. A silken carpet is laid out over the marble floor. The guest of honor sits to the east, the direction associated with the sun god Ra, while everyone else gathers around to form a circle. In the center is a large silver serving tray. Sheep's brains—white in color and similar in consistency to a light tofu—are the first course; they are carried in from the kitchen in stately fashion and served first to the guest of honor. After this comes couscous, a dish of grain and stew common to most Mediterranean countries, particularly those of North Africa. Meat and vegetable kebabs, roasted and served on skewers, are accompanied by a thin bread. Alongside a stew in a ceramic pot is a nest of aromatic grasses with a pigeon at the center, followed by green soup and topped off with strong, flavorful coffee or mint tea.

Diners eat with their hands, occasionally washing them in water. The host personally serves the dishes to his invited guests. Rose petals float in the water glasses. (Originally it was an Arab custom to reward visitors coming from long distances with rosewater.) Young girls in rainbow-colored costumes dance. Soon it is daybreak, and voices calling the people to morning prayer fill the air. (Yukiko Tanizawa)

LE MAROCAIN
Hotel La Mamounia
Avenue Bab Jdid, Marrakech, Morocco
Tel: (04)48981 Fax: (04)44940 Telex: 72018
日本事務所：B

1,5：アラブ文化圏特有の漆喰装飾ゲブスがレストラン内部を飾る。スタッフのコスチュームもモロッコの民族衣装。2：パティオを囲んだレストラン・スペースも設けられている。3：23年間、このレストランのシェフを勤めるベラダ・アジサ女史。母親もこのレストランの先代シェフだった。料理は「ジャジュ・ムシャルメル」と呼ばれる鳥のレモン・ソース。ワインはモロッコ産のゲルワン。食器はフランス製のピリヴュ焼。4：北アフリカ、モロッコを代表するホテルである。

●●●

1, 5: Traditional Arabic "Gebs" scrolled plasterwork decorates the restaurant interior. The staff uniforms are traditional Moroccan folk costumes. 2: One section of the restaurant surrounds a small roofed patio. 3: Berrada L'Aziza has been chef here for 23 years, and her mother worked as chef before her. Chicken in lemon sauce (*djaj m'charmel*) is a typical dish. Moroccan Guerrouane wine is served, and the china is from Pillivuyt in France. 4: This is a typical Moroccan hotel in many ways.

3

4

MARRAKECH L'IMPERIALE
Hotel La Mamounia
Avenue Bab Jdid, Marrakech, Morocco
Tel: (04)48981 Fax: (04)44940 Telex: 72018
日本事務所：B

1,2: このレストランは、パリのミシュラン三つ星のレストラン「リュカ・キャルトン」のシェフ、アラン・サンドランスの料理を受け継いでいる。昼食はビュッフェも提供される。3: マラケシュの町を描いた18枚の油絵と、ジャック・マジョレル作の天井画で装飾。4: ホテル・ラ・マムーニャには6つのレストランがあり、そのメイン・ダイニングが「マラケシュ・アンペリアル」。

•••

1, 2: At midday a luncheon buffet is served. The French cuisine here is prepared according to the recipes of chef Alain Senderens of the three-stars restaurant *Lucas Carton* in Paris. 3: Eighteen paintings of the city of Marrakech hang from the walls. The ceiling fresco is the work of Jacques Majorelle. 4: Hotel La Mamounia has six restaurants; *Marrakech l'Imperiale* serves as the main dining room.

AL FASSIA
Hotel Palais Jamai
Bab El Guissa, Fez, Morocco
Tel:(06)343-31 Fax:(06)350-96
Telex:51974/51977
日本事務所：B

1, 3, 7：モロッコ料理のレストラン「アル・フェッシア」は、内部がいくつもの小部屋に分けられ、民族音楽や舞踊も楽しめる。70席。**2, 4**：メニューの表紙はモロッコの古都フェズの風景。**5**：骨付きの鳩肉とアーモンド入りのパイ。**6**：モロッコの伝統料理、仔ヒツジの肉と野菜のクスクス。ポーションが大きいのは、主人が食べたあと、使用人に分け与えた昔の名残りという。

■■■

1, 3, 7: The Moroccan reestaurant *Al Fassia* seats 70 diners, with the interior divided into a number of small rooms. Patrons can enjoy traditional Moroccan folk music and dance while they dine. **2, 4:** The menu cover shows a view of the town of Fez. This hotel is located in the old Moroccan capital of Fez. **5:** Puff pastry stuffed with pigeon and almonds (*feuilleté farci de pigeons et d'amandes*). **6:** A traditional Moroccan dish, couscous with lamb and vegetables (*couscous aux sept légumes*). The large-sized portions are a remnant of a long-ago custom: After the master had finished eating he would divide the remaining food among his servants.

2

LA DJENINA
Hotel Palais Jamai
Bab El Guissa, Fez, Morocco
Tel: (06)343-31 Fax: (06)350-96
Telex: 51974/51977
日本事務所：B

1：ホテル・パレ・ジャマイのメイン・ダイニングは、フランス料理をベースとしたインターナショナル・レストラン「ラ・ジェニナ」。エグゼクティブ・シェフは仏人パトリック・ブリアン。光沢タイル装飾（ゼリージ）の柱、アラベスク文様の木製天井でコーディネートされている。2：ホテルのロゴ・マークが入った食器、ナプキン、グラス、灰皿。3：屋外テラスは、主に昼食に用いられ、古都フェズが眺望できる。屋内屋外合わせて200席。

●●●

1: *La Djenina*, the main dining room of Hotel Palais Jamai, is an international restaurant serving mainly French cuisine. The executive chef is Frenchman Patrick Briand. The interior features "Zelliges" glazed tile columns and an "Arabesque" design wooden ceiling. 2: The hotel's crest is incorporated in the design of the plates, napkins, glasses and ashtrays. 3: The outdoor terrace area, mainly used at lunchtime, offers a view of Fez, the old capital. Including both indoor and outdoor areas, some 200 diners can be accommodated.

3

CITADEL GRILL
Ramses Hilton
1115 Corniche El Nile, Cairo, Egypt
Tel:(2)744400/758000 Fax:(2)757152
日本事務所：G

1,2:「ガーデン・コート・ラウンジ」を見下すアトリウムの出窓内部に席を設けたレストラン「シタデル・グリル」はコンチネンタル料理を提供。また、「エジプシャン・コーナー」ではエジプトのア・ラ・カルト料理も楽しめる。同名のバーも付設されている。
3: カイロ市内を流れるナイル川沿いに建てられた35階の高層ホテル、ラムセス・ヒルトンの開業は、1981年5月。

●●●

1, 2: Atrium bay windows look out over the *Garden Court Lounge*; inside the windows is seating for the *Citadel Grill* restaurant. The specialty here is Continental cuisine, and there's also a bar. Egyptian dishes are served à la carte in the special "Egyptian Corner." 3: The Ramses Hilton, named after an ancient Egyptian king, opened in May, 1981. The 35-story high-rise hotel stands on the banks of the Nile as it flows through Cairo.

KING TUT GRILL
Heliopolis Sheraton Hotel & Towers
Uruba St, Heliopolis, Cairo, Egypt
Tel: 665500/667700 Fax: (202)2907546
日本事務所：T

1：カイロ国際空港の西部は、古代エジプト時代にヘリオポリスと呼ばれた地域。ここに1979年10月に開業したのがヘリオポリス・シェラトン・ホテル・アンド・タワーズ。2：ツタンカーメン王の頭文字を冠した美食料理のレストラン「キング・トゥート・グリル」の中央には、ファラオが死後の世界で使用する"太陽の船"が飾られている。

1: The area west of Cairo International Airport was known in ancient times as Heliopolis, and it is here that the Heliopolis Sheraton Hotel & Towers opened in October, 1979. 2: In 1922 in the "Valley of the kings," English archeologist Howard Carter discovered the tomb of the boy king, Tutankhamnen, after whom this popular gourmet restaurant is named. In the center of the *King Tut Grill* is a "Solar Boat," representing the craft used by the king in his travels in the afterlife.

TURKISH COFFEE CORNER
Holiday Inn Shinx
P.O.Box 45, Giza, Pyramids, Egypt
Tel:854700, 854930 Telex:94097 HOLIN UN
日本事務所：D

1：濃厚なトルコ・コーヒーを提供する「ターキッシュ・コーヒー・コーナー」。コーヒーは近世までは中東を中心とした飲物だった。2：ギザの三大ピラミッドを望む好立地の低層ホテル。コーヒー・ショップ「ランデヴー」、アイスクリーム・パーラー「ペンギン」、レストラン「グリル・ルーム」などの飲食施設が、ロビー奥の大廊下に設けられている。

●●●

1: The *Turkish Coffee Corner*, serving strong Turkish coffee brewed from heavily roasted beans, reminds us of the important role played by coffee in Middle Eastern history. **2:** This low-rise hotel looks out over the three great pyramids of Giza. The long hall at the end of the lobby leads to the *Rendezvous* coffee shop, *Penguin* ice cream parlour and *Grill Room* restaurant.

LA MAMMA
Cairo Sheraton Hotel, Casino & Towers
Galaa Square, Giza, Cairo, Egypt
Tel:3488600/3488700 Fax:(202)3489051
日本事務所：T

1：ナイル河のゲジラ島とローダ島を望むカジノ・ホテル。最上階の46室とスイート・ルームを、特別なサービスが受けられるタワーズとして区別している。
2,3：3階にあるイタリア料理のレストラン「ラ・マンマ」。昼から深夜2時までの営業で、昼食時はビュッフェも楽しめる。ナイルを眺望できるレストランとして人気を呼んでいる。

1: This casino hotel stands on the left bank of the Nile, looking out over Gezirah Island and Roda Island. The hotel provides a special class of "Towers" service for the guests in the 46 rooms and suites on the top floor. 2, 3: *La Mamma*, on the third floor, is a popular Italian restaurant looking out on the Nile. It is open from lunchtime until 2:00 a.m., and serves a buffet luncheon at midday.

AMERICA

アメリカ合衆国：祖国を抱いた新大陸

　一つの国……と呼ぶにはあまりにも広大なアメリカ。東側では、メイフラワー号の移住以来、アングロ・サクソンが文化の主流をなしてきた。その後加わった他の人種も、それぞれ祖国を背負って暮らしてきた。根深い階級意識、躾のきびしさ、伝統の尊重は、良くも悪くも古いヨーロッパを継承しているのだろう。一つ、食事はフランス料理をよしとする。上流社会はフランス語を話し、フランス料理を食べることになっているからだ。

　西は、開拓の過程で、体力が教養を、自由が因習を、協調が自己主張を上まわる時代が長かった。料理は、大鍋で始まっている。出身地の自慢料理も、鍋のなかに溶けている。また、ポーク＆ビーンズ（豚肉と豆の煮込み）から家族の団欒を連想する人も多いはず。ミシシッピー流域から南部では、ナマズやワニもレストランのメニューに堂々登場してくる。ともにフライが多いが、もとの姿さえ想像しなければ、結構おいしい。

〔谷沢由起子〕

United States of America: A Mirror of Many Homelands

　Although it is a single country, the U.S. stretches across an entire continent and embraces many cultures. On the east coast, immigrants arriving on the Mayflower brought along Anglo-Saxon traditions while settlers from other lands brought with them the ways of their various homelands. For better or worse, they also inherited from the Old World of Europe a way of thinking which included deep-rooted class consciousness, strict educational methods and respect for tradition. France and French cooking were highly admired, and in upper-class society French was spoken and French cuisine was served.

　Out west, while the frontier was being tamed there was a long period during which strong bodies were more important than educated minds, freedom was more important than conventionality, and cooperation more important than self-assertiveness. Cooking was done in a big pot, and here were gathered and blended together the favorite dishes of a number of homelands. Today the basic one-pot dish, "pork and beans," brings to mind images of happy family group to many people. Here in the west even such humble items as catfish and alligator from the Mississippi delta appear in dignified fashion on restaurant menus. Usually served fried, they're actually quite tasty as long as one doesn't think too much about their original appearance.

(Yukiko Tanizawa)

1

2

3

Great Hotels of the World: vol. 5 — 77

4

5

6

7

9

8

SEASHELL
Coco Palms Resort
P.O.Box 631, Lihue, Kauai,
Hawaii 86766 U.S.A.
Tel:808-822-4921 Telex:743-1304 COCOH
日本事務所：O

1：カウアイ島の女王デボラ・カプレの宮殿跡に建てられたポリネシアン・クラシック・ホテル。2-11：ビーチ寄りに離れて建つ「シーシェル」レストラン。エグゼクティブ・シェフはJ・M・ジョスラン。ブリュッセル・ヒルトン、ニュー・オーリンズのセント・ルイス・ホテル、ホテル・ハナ・マウイなどを経て当ホテルに就任し、ハワイ風の創作料理を完成した。9：タロイモのフェットゥチーネ、ロブスター添え。10：地鶏の胸肉マリネ・グリル。11：蒸しパンではさんだポルトガル・ソーセージのグリル、中国マスタード味。

●●●

1: This "Polynesian Classic" hotel was built on the original site of the royal palace of Deborar Kapule, the queen of Kauai Island. 2-11: *Seashell* restaurant occupies its own beachside building, separate from the hotel wing. The executive chef, Jean-Marie Josselin, worked at the Brussels Hilton, the Saint Louis Hotel in New Orleans, and the Hotel Hana Maui before coming here. His repertoire includes a number of original Hawaiian-style dishes. 9: Taro fettucine with lobster. 10: Grilled marinated island breast of chicken. 11: Grilled Portuguese sausage with steamed bread and Chinese mustard.

10

11

1

2

MONARCH ROOM
The Royal Hawaiian Hotel
2259 Kalakaua Ave,
Honolulu, Hawaii 96815 U.S.A.
Tel:808-923-7311 Fax:808-924-7098
日本事務所：T

1：オワフ島のワイキキ海岸に建つロイヤル・ハワイアン・ホテル。別名"ピンク・パレス"。ショーが楽しめる1947年完成のレストランが「モナーク・ルーム」。開業時には、ここにアラブ風装飾で飾られたメイン・ダイニング「パージャン・ルーム」が置かれていた。1945年からのホテルの全面改装で、現在の「モナーク・ルーム」が完成した。2：メニューにもピンク・パレスがデザインされている。

●●●

1: The Royal Hawaiian Hotel, nicknamed the "Pink Palace," is on Waikiki Beach on the island of Oahu. The *Monarch Room* restaurant, featuring dinner shows, opened in 1947. Originally this area was the hotel's main dining room, the *Persian Room*, decorated in Arabic style and dating back to the hotel's opening in 1927. *The Monarch Room* was added during the renovation of the hotel which began in 1945. 2: The menu features a "Pink Palace" design.

1

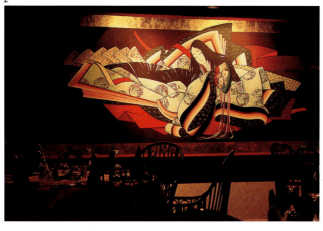

2

3

MIDORI
Kauai Hilton & Beach Villas
4331 Kauai Beach Drive,
Lihue, Kauai, Hawaii 86766 U.S.A.
Tel: (808)245-1955 Fax: (808)246-9085
日本事務所：F

1,2：メイン・ダイニング「ミドリ」は、コンチネンタル料理を提供するレストラン。80席。内部は日本画で飾られ、レストランの名称を示した緑色のイタリア大理石で装飾されている。おすすめ料理は、「タロイモのクリーム・スープ」、「ロブスターの天ぷら」など。ハワイならではの料理が楽しめる。3：カウアイ島のリフエ空港からわずか10分のリゾート・ホテル。

1, 2: The main dining room, *Midori*, serves Continental cuisine and seats 80. The interior features classic Japanese paintings and green Italian marble. (The name, *Midori*, means "green" in Japanese.) Among the specialties are a number of uniquely Hawaiian dishes such as cream of taro soup and lobster tempura. 3: This resort hotel is ten minutes from Lihue Airport on the island of Kauai.

PARC CAFE
Waikiki Parc Hotel
2233 Helumoa Road,
Honolulu, Hawaii 96815 U.S.A.
Tel:(808)921-7272 Fax:(808)923-1336
日本事務所：A

1,3,4：「パーク・カフェ」は、コンチネンタル料理、アメリカ料理を提供するレストラン。132席。ハワイ特有の生ジュースを使った朝食の「セット・メニュー」が楽しめる。リーズナブルな料金の優良ホテルとして知られている。2：ワイキキ海岸に1987年11月1日開業した298室、22階建のホテル。隣接するハレクラニ・ホテルを所有するハレクラニ・コーポレーションが開発運営している。

●●●

1, 3, 4: The *Parc Cafe*, with seating for 132, serves Continental and American cuisine. The breakfast set menu includes fresh Hawaiian fruit juices. The hotel has a reputation for providing good accommodations at reasonable prices. 2: This 22-story, 298-room hotel opened on Waikiki Beach in 1st November 1987. It was built and managed by Halekulani Corporation, which also owns the adjacent Halekulani Hotel.

1

2

KACHO
Waikiki Parc Hotel
2233 Helumoa Road,
Honolulu, Hawaii 96815 U.S.A.
Tel:(808)921-7272 Fax:(808)923-1336
日本事務所：A

1：写真手前が「花鳥朝食」。小付、小鉢、焼物、煮物、生玉子、お新香、海苔、味噌汁、御飯で構成される日本の代表的な朝食。焼物はアジの開き。写真奥の「朝粥朝食」もある純日本式のレストラン。2：日本料理レストラン「花鳥」は朝・昼・夜食を提供し、寿司カウンターもある。40席。

1: Shown in the foreground is the "Kacho Breakfast," a typical Japanese breakfast including seafood appetizer, vegetable appetizer, broiled fish, braised vegetables, raw egg, pickled vegetables, seaweed, miso soup and rice. The broiled fish is *aji* (horse mackerel). At the back is the "Asakayu Breakfast," featuring rice porridge. The restaurant is also popular among non-Japanese guests for its authentic Japanese cuisine. 2: *Kacho* Japanese restaurant has seating for 40 and includes a sushi bar. The restaurant, which serves breakfast, lunch and dinner, was provided for the hotel's many Japanese guests.

1

2

SILK'S
Mandarin Oriental, San Francisco
222 Sansoome Street,
San Francisco, California 94104-2792 U.S.A.
Tel:(415)885-0999 Fax:(415)433-0289
Telex:5106001025
日本事務所：L

1,2：レストラン「シルクス」は、フランス料理をベースとしたカリフォルニア料理店。左からシェフのデビッド・キンチ、エグゼクティブ・シェフのリチャード・ホフ。ワインはカリフォルニア産。テーブル上の赤ワインはモンダヴィ・ロスチャイルド・1984年。白ワインは、シャルドネイ・1987年。食器は、ヴィレロイ・アンド・ボッホ焼、アルコ・パターン・デザイン。3,4：サンフランシスコの金融街の高層ビル上部に開業したホテルだが、ホテル専用の入口がある。5：ロブスター・サラダのカレー風味、アスパラガス添え。6：日本産焼マグロ、マンゴーとオレンジ・バター風味。7：チョコレート・ケーキ。

1, 2: *Silk's* restaurant specializes in a style of California cuisine adapted from French cooking. From left: Chef David Kinch, Executive Chef Richard Hoff. The wine is from California: shown on the table is Opus One Mondavi Rothschild 1984 (red) and Mount Eden Vineyards Estate Chardonnay 1987 (white). The Arco pattern servingware is by Villeroy & Boch. 3, 4: This hotel occupies the upper floors of a skyscraper in San Francisco's financial district. It has its own separate entrance. 5: Curried lobster salad with fresh asparagus. 6: Seared Japanese tuna with mango relish and orange butter. 7: Flourless chocolate cake with coffee sauce.

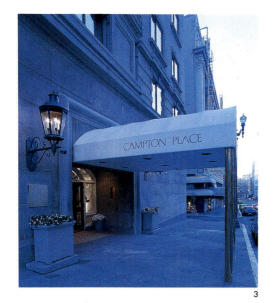

3

4

CAMPTON PLACE RESTAURANT
Campton Place Hotel
340 Stockton Street,
San Francisco, California 94108 U.S.A.
Tel:(415)781-5555 Fax:(415)955-8536
日本事務所：B

1,2,4: 革新的なアメリカ料理を提供する「キャンプトン・プレイス・レストラン」。68席。食器はウエッジウッド焼、伊万里・デザイン。3: サンフランシスコのユニオン・スクエアーに隣接するラクシャリー・ホテル。5: 軽く燻したマスとライム味の岩エビ。6: チョコレートのシャーベット、ラズベリー添え。7: エグゼクティブ・シェフはジャン・I・バーンボーム。ルイジアナ州バトン・ルージュ生れ。ニュー・オーリンズ発祥のスパイシー料理（ケージュン料理）を提供する「K・ポールズ・ルイジアナ・キッチン」で修業。ニューヨークのレストラン「クイルテッド・ジラフ」のヘッド・シェフなどを経て、当レストランのエグゼクティブ・シェフに就任。

1, 2, 4: *Campton Place Restaurant* serves a novel style of American cuisine. The serving-ware is Imari design Wedgwood china. 3: This luxury hotel overlooks Union Square in San Francisco. 5: Lightly smoked lake trout with lime-marinated rock shrimp. 6: Pistachio tulip with chocolate sherbet and raspberries. 7: Executive chef Jan I. Birnbaum was born in Baton Rouge, Louisiana, and trained at *K-Paul's Louisiana Kitchen*, which specializes in Cajun cuisine. He was head chef at New York's famous *Quilted Giraffe* before coming here.

5

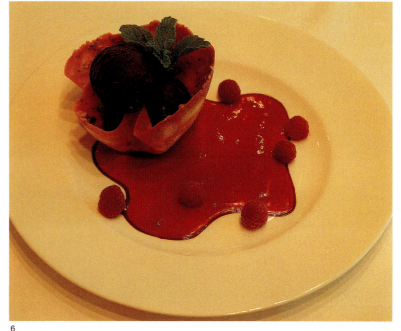

6

7

Great Hotels of the World: vol. 5 — 87

THE GARDEN COURT
The Sheraton-Palace Hotel
2 New Montgomery St., San Francisco
94105 California U.S.A.
Tel: 415-392-8600 Fax: 415-543-0671
日本事務所：T

1–3: 世界で最も美しいダイニング・ルームと評価される「ザ・ガーデン・コート」。朝・昼食を提供。夜はパーティーや宴会場として使われる。サンフランシスコ大地震（1906年）で被害を受ける前には、ここは馬車を乗り入れるエントランスだった。1991年春、ホテルはリノヴェーションを終了し、古い部分を再生させた。写真はリノヴェーション以前の状況。4: 西海岸最初の大型ホテル（800室）として1875年10月に開業したアメリカのグランド・ホテルのひとつ。

1–3: *The Garden Court* is often praised as the most beautiful dining room in the world. Breakfast and lunch are served, and in the evenings it is used for banquets and parties. Before the hotel was damaged in the San Francisco Earthquake of 1906, this area was used as an entrance for horse-drawn carriages. Renovation and restoration work was completed in the spring of 1991; the photographs show the restaurant's pre-renovation appearance. 4: At the time of its opening in October 1875, this 800-room "Grand Hotel" was the first large-scale hotel on the American west coast.

WELLINGTON'S
San Francisco Marriort Fisherman's Wharf
1250 Columbus Avenue, San Francisco
94133 California U.S.A.
Tel:(415)775-7555 Fax:(415)474-2099
日本事務所：K

1,3 カリフォルニア料理のレストラン「ウエリントンズ」は新鮮なシーフードを提供する。朝・昼・夕食それぞれのビュッフェも用意され深夜まで営業。また日曜日のランチョンには豊富な魚介類が楽しめる。2：サンフランシスコの観光地フイッシャーマンズ・ウォーフ近くの4階建のホテル。256室。増大する観光客をターゲットに開発された。

1, 3: *Wellington's* specializes in fresh seafood and California cuisine. Breakfast, lunch and dinner buffets are served, and the restaurant stays open until late at night. A wide assortment of fish and seafood is served at Sunday luncheon. 2: This 4-story, 256-room hotel was built near one of San Francisco's most popular tourist destinations, Fisherman's Wharf, and was developed in response to increased tourism in the city.

1

2

THE BEACON
Hyatt Regency Long Beach
200 South Pine Avenue, Long Beach
California 90802 U.S.A.
Tel: 213-491-1234 Fax: 213-432-1972
日本事務所：E

1:「ザ・ビーコン（灯台）」は、内部に灯台をデザインしたユニークな「ビーコン・ラウンジ」を付帯する美食レストラン。ダウン・タウンのJ桟橋に繋留された豪華客船クィーン・メリー号などが眺望できる。2: ロサンジェルス南郊の港町ロング・ビーチにある総ガラス張りの近代的ホテル。521室。コンベンション・アンド・エンターテインメント・センターに隣接している。

●●●

1: The uniquely designed *Beacon Lounge* is part of *The Beacon* restaurant. The restaurant is known for its excellent food, and it offers a view of the *Queen Mary*, the luxury cruise ship now docked at Pier J near downtown Long Beach. 2: This modern, glass-walled hotel is located in Long Beach, a port city serving Los Angeles. It has 521 guest rooms and stands next to the city's Convention and Entertainment Center.

92 ——— AMERICA

3

4

CHECKERS RESTAURANT
Checkers Hotel
535 South Grand Avenue,
Los Angeles, California 90071 U.S.A.
Tel:(213)624-0000 Fax:(213)626-9906
日本事務所：B

1,2：エグゼクティブ・シェフはジェリー・カンファート。カリフォルニア・ワインの産地ナパ・ヴァレイのレストラン「ドーマン・シャンドン」、サンフランシスコのスタンフォード・コート・ホテルのレストラン「フールノーズ・オーヴンズ」などを経て現職。食器はウエッジウッド焼、伊万里・デザイン。カンファートの銘柄ワイン（ピノ・ノアール・アンド・シャルドネイ）も提供される。チェッカーズ式の革新的アメリカ料理のレストランとして知られている。3：前身はロサンジェルス最初のヨーロッパ調ホテル、メイフラワー・ホテル。4：レストラン入口に置かれたマスコットの鍍金製木彫像"インディアン・ボーイ"。5：ズッキーニの花をあしらった鶏肉のグリル。6：サーモンのグリル、長ネギの漉し汁ソース。7：ロブスターとポテト、トマトとメボウキ（シソ科の一年草、はっかに似た香を持つ）・ソース。アメリカ独特の料理のひとつ。

●●●

1, 2: Before coming here, executive chef Jerry Comfort worked at *Domaine Chandon* in northern California's wine-producing Napa Valley, and at *Fournou's Ovens* in San Francisco's Stanford Court Hotel. Wedgwood Imari servingware is used. Wine (Pinot Noir and Chardonnay) bearing Jerry Comfort's own label is served, as is beer. The restaurant is known for its unique, "Checkers-style" American cuisine. 3: This was originally known as the Mayflower Hotel, the first European-style hotel to be built in Los Angeles. 4: Standing at the entrance is a gilt wooden statue of an Indian boy. 5: Free-range chicken stuffed with homemade ricotta, served with zucchini blossom fritters and sweet pea mash. 6: Grilled salmon wrapped in bacon with spring onion puree and golden hominy. 7: Lobster-stuffed potato with spring peas, tomato and basil. The cuisine here is uniquely American.

5

6

7

1

2

RAVEL
Sheraton Grande Hotel
333 South Figueroa Street,
Los Angeles, California 90071 U.S.A.
Tel: (213)617-1133 Fax:(213)613-0291
日本事務所：T

1,3: 1階のレストラン「ラヴェル」は、1930年代に黄金期のハリウッド映画産業が招いた作曲家モーリス・ラヴェルを記念して命名。内部はエッチング・ガラスで飾られ、オリジナルのアメリカ料理、フランス料理を提供。96席。2: バンカー・ヒル都市再開発プロジェクトの一環としてロサンジェルスの金融街に建てられ、1983年に開業。470室。14階建、総ミラー・ガラス張りのホテル。

●●●

1, 3: In the 1930's, during the "Golden Age of Hollywood," French composer Maurice Ravel was invited to write music for the movies; it is after him that the first-floor restaurant *Ravel* is named. Etched glass decorates the interior of the restaurant, which seats 96. French cuisine and original American cuisine are the specialties. 2: This modern hotel, covered in mirrored glass, opened in 1983 in the Los Angeles financial district. The 14-story, 470-room facility was built as part of the Bunker Hill Urban Renewal Project.

3

1

2

HASTING'S
The Anaheim Hilton & Towers
777 Convention Way, Anaheim,
California 92802-3497 U.S.A.
Tel: (714)740-4250 Telex: 183-286
日本事務所：F

1：6つのレストランのうち、メイン・ダイニングとして機能する近代フランス料理・コンチネンタル料理のレストラン「ヘースティングズ」。同名の「ヘースティングズ・バー」も付属している。2：ディズニーランドのある街として著名なロサンジェルス南東部アナハイムのコンベンション・センターの裏手に1984年5月開業した、1,600室の大型ホテル。

●●●

1: One of the hotel's six restaurants, *Hasting's* serves modern French and Continental cuisine and functions as the main dining room. *Hasting's Bar* is inside. 2: Anaheim, southeast of Los Angeles, is best known as the home of Disneyland. This huge, 1600-room hotel opened in May 1984 behind the Anaheim Convention Center.

CARDINI
Los Angeles Hilton & Towers
930 Wilshire Boulevard, Los Angeles,
California 90017 U.S.A.
Tel:(213)629-4321
日本事務所：F

1-5: 1985年開店の北イタリア料理のレストラン「カルディーニ」。地中海をイメージしたブルーとグレイ・カラーでコーディネート。長い廊下を配し、2ヵ所の小さなダイニング部（ミニ・ダイニング・ルーム）で構成。80年代中期、アメリカのチェーン・ホテルでは、北イタリア料理レストランを開店させるのがひとつの流行だった。**2:** 1952年にスタットラー・ホテルからキャピトル・ヒルトンに改称。1968年にさらにロサンジェルス・ヒルトンと改名。1987年、当時の金額で100億円をかけたリノヴェーションが完了。

●●●

1–5: This northern Italian restaurant opened in 1985. The interior displays a Mediterranean color scheme of muted blues and grays, and the restaurant includes two mini-dining rooms at the end of a long corridor. This is just one of the many northern Italian restaurants opened by hotel chains during the peak of their popularity in the mid-1980's. **2:** In 1952 the original Statler Hotel was renamed the Capitol Hilton, and in 1968 it became the Los Angeles Hilton. The current hotel was completed in 1987 after renovation work costing $60 million.

Great Hotels of the World: vol.5 ——— 97

MELROSE
Park Hyatt Washington, D.C.
24th at M Street, N.W.
Washington, D.C. 20037 U.S.A.
Tel:(202)789-1234 Fax:(202)457-8823
Telex:897105
日本事務所：E

1,5：レストラン「メルローズ」は、創作アメリカ料理を提供する当市でも人気のレストラン。食器はヴィレロイ・アンド・ボッホ焼、シエナ・マーブル・デザイン。2：アメリカの首都ワシントン・D.C.に1986年開業したハイアット社の最高級カテゴリー、パーク・ハイアットのひとつ。3,4：レストランに付設する「ザ・ラウンジ」。6-8：クラブ・スタイルの「ザ・バー」を付帯し、屋外テラス「ザ・カフェ」も置かれている。メニューは毎日変えられる。

3

4

5

6

1, 5: *Melrose* is popular among Washingtonians as well as hotel guests for its original American cuisine. The servingware is Sienna marble design by Villeroy & Boch. 2: Park Hyatt is the name given to the Hyatt Corporation's top class of hotels; this one, in Washington, D.C., opened in 1986. 3, 4: *The Lounge* is also part of the restaurant. 6–8: Included here are a club-style bar, *The Bar*, and an outdoor terrace, *The Cafe*. The menu changes daily depending on the availability of fresh ingredients.

7

8

Great Hotels of the World: vol. 5 — 99

9

10

12

11

9：レモン・フラン（パイの一種）、新鮮な季節のベリー添え。ラズベリー、ブルーベリー、ストロベリーに、チョコレートで線をデザイン。10：冷たいスフレ、チョコレート・ソース。11：チョコレート・アーモンド・ケーキ。チョコレートで襞をデザイン。12：パストリイ・シェフのピーター・ブレッド。ワシントン・D.C.のヒルトン・ホテルなどで修業し、当レストランでオリジナル・ケーキを創作。13：エグゼクティブ・スー・シェフのジェラード・E・トンプソン。ヒューストンのリッツ・カールトン・ホテルを経て当レストランに。14：ドーバー・ソール（シタビラメ）のグリル、ローストした甘唐辛子とレタス添え。15：ソフト・シェル・クラブ、ヴァージニア・ハムとコーン添え。ソフト・シェル・クラブは脱皮直後の殻の軟かい食用ガニ、この地方の名物。16：マグロのカルパッチョ、パルメザン・チーズ添え、ペスト・ソース。カルパッチョは本来、生の牛肉をスライスしてソースをかけた料理。ペスト・ソースは、バジリコ、ニンニク、オリーブ油で作るパスタ用のソースである。白い食器はヴィレロイ・アンド・ボッホ焼、デルタ・デザイン。

14

13

15

16

9: Lemon flan with seasonal fresh berries and chocolate lace. Raspberries, blueberries, and strawberries are used, depending on the season. **10:** Frozen Grand Marnier souffle with white and dark chocolate sauces. **11:** Flourless chocolate and almond cake with hard chocolate ruffles. **12:** Pastry chef Peter Brett makes a number of original cakes and pastries. He trained at the Washington, D.C. Hilton. **13:** Executive sous-chef Gerard E. Thompson worked at the Ritz-Carlton Hotel in Houston before coming here. **14:** Grilled Dover sole with roast sweet peppers and lamb's lettuce. **15:** Soft-shell crabs with Virginia ham and sweet corn. Soft-shell crabs are a local favorite dish. **16:** Ahi tuna carpaccio with shaved Rocca parmesan and two pestos. ("Carpaccio" originally refers to thinly sliced raw beef served with a sauce. Pesto sauce is made from crushed basil, garlic, olive oil and other ingredients, and is usually served with pasta.) Delta pattern, white Villeroy & Boch servingware is used.

WILLARD ROOM
The Willard Inter·Continental
1401, Pennsylvania Avenue, N.W.
Washington, D.C. 20004 U.S.A.
Tel:(202)628-9100 Fax:(202)637-7307
Telex:897-099
日本事務所：H

1, 2：アメリカ料理を提供するレストラン「ザ・ウイラード・ルーム」は、インテリアを初期19世紀様式でコーディネート。食器はヴィレロイ・アンド・ボッホ焼。ロビーのモザイク・タイル・フロアーにもデザインされたホテルの頭文字"W"を絵付けした特注品。3：アメリカの首都のランドマーク・ホテルで、ホワイト・ハウスに隣接。"大統領たちの館"の異名がある。

1, 2: *The Willard Room* restaurant serves American cuisine. The interior is decorated in early 19th century style, and the servingware is by Villeroy & Boch, with the hotel's initial, "W," in its design. **3:** This landmark hotel is near the White House in Washington, D.C. It has the nickname "The Presidential Palace."

1

2

3

BULL & BEAR
The Waldorf=Astoria & Towers
—A Hilton Hotel

50th Street & Park Avenue,
New York, New York 10022 U.S.A.
Tel: (212)355-3000 Fax: (212)872-6380
Telex: 666747
日本事務所：F

1：最後のグランド・ホテルといわれるニュー・ヨークの名門ホテル。2：レストラン「ブル・アンド・ベアー」は、サンドイッチからシーフード、ステーキまで幅広くアメリカ料理を提供、同名の「バー」を付帯する。以前は"メンズ・クラブ"として機能していた。3：フォーク、ナイフにまで雄牛と熊のユニークなデザインが取り入れられている。

●●●

1: This illustrious New York hotel is sometimes called "the last Grand Hotel." 2: The *Bull & Bear* restaurant has its own bar and serves a wide variety of American dishes ranging from sandwiches to steak and seafood. A men's club once occupied this site. The name "Bull & Bear" refers to buyers and sellers on the stock market. 3: A unique "bull and bear" motif is incorporated in the design of the plates and silverware.

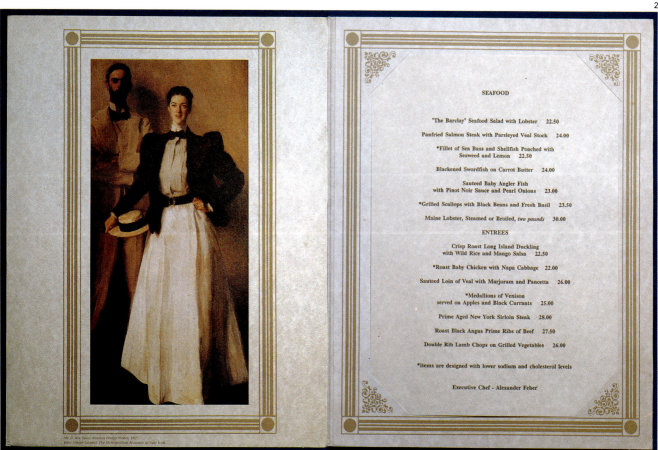

THE BARCLEY
Hotel Inter·Continental New York
111 East 48 Street,
New York, New York 10017 U.S.A.
Tel:(212)755-5900　Fax:(212)644-0079
Telex:968677
日本事務所：H

1：レストラン・マネージャーのヨセフ・ヴィジアーニ（写真：左）とエグゼクティブ・シェフのアレグザンダー・フェハー。フェハーは、中東、ヨーロッパのホテル・インター・コンチネンタルで修業して、1983年から当ホテルに就任。2：レストランの壁を飾るのは英国の科学者・数学者アイザック・ニュートン夫妻の肖像画。同じ画像がメニューの表紙にも使われている。3：レストランの名称は、ホテルの前身ザ・バークリー・ホテルから取られている。4：ドーバー・ソール（シタビラメ）のスフレ、小エビ添え。5：鶉のグリル、レンズ豆とアスパラガス添え。6：ズッキーニの花とキノコの温野菜。

●●●

1: (From left) restaurant manager Joseph A. Viggiani and executive chef Alexander Feher. Chef Feher trained at Inter·Continental hotels in Europe and the Middle East before coming here in 1983. **2:** A portrait of English mathematician Sir Isaac Newton (1642–1727) and his wife hangs from the wall. The same portrait is also on the cover of the menu. **3:** This hotel has its origins in *The Barcley Hotel,* from which *The Barcley* restaurant takes its name. **4:** Soufflé of Dover sole with tarragon vinaigrette. **5:** Grilled quail with green lentils. **6:** Zucchini blossoms with mushroom coulis.

MAURICE
Parker Meridien New York
118, West 57th Street,
New York, New York 10019 U.S.A.
Tel:(212)245-5000 Telex:6801134
日本事務所：M

1,3: レストラン「モーリス」は、パリのミシュラン三つ星レストラン「リュカ・キャルトン」のシェフ、アラン・サンドランスの流れを汲み、新フランス料理を提供する。食器はヴィレロイ・アンド・ボッホ焼。レストランの名称は、ワインと女性を愛したフランス人歌手・映画俳優のモーリス・シュヴァリエ(1888〜1972年)にちなんでいる。2: ニュー・ヨークのセントラル・パーク近くに1984年開業した高層ホテル。41階建、579室、97室のアパートメントを付帯している。

1, 3: Restaurant *Maurice* serves French nouvelle cuisine, following the cooking methods originated by Alain Senderens, chef at the Michelin three-star restauarant *Lucas Carton* in Paris. The servingware is by Villeroy & Boch. The restaurant is named after French singer, actor and bon vivant Maurice Chevalier (1888–1972). 2: This high-rise hotel opened in 1984 near Central Park in New York. It has 41 stories, 579 guest rooms and 97 apartments.

1

2

DEVEREUX'S
Essex House
160 Central Park South, New York,
New York 10019 U.S.A.
Tel: (212) 247-0300 Fax: (212) 315-1839
日本事務所：N

1：コンチネンタル料理のレストラン「デヴローズ」には、バー「ザ・ウインドジャマー（帆船）」がある。日曜日には"サンデー・ブランチ"が楽しめる。2：セントラル・パーク南端に立つ40階建のホテル。開業は1931年10月、エンパイアー・ステイト・ビルディングと同時であった。702室。1985年7月12日、日本航空が全額出資するホテル運営会社ニッコー・ホテルズ・インターナショナルが買収。

●●●

1: *Devereux's* restaurant specializes in Continental cuisine and includes a bar, *The Windjammer*. Brunch is served on Sundays. 2: This 40-story, 702-room hotel at the south end of New York's Central Park opened in October 1931, the same month as the Empire State Building. In 1985 it was bought by Nikko Hotels International, a hotel management company owned by Japan Air Lines.

3

4

5

6

7

8

WINDOWS
Marriott Suites Chicago O'Hare
6155 North River Road,
Rosemont, Illinois 60018 U.S.A.
Tel: (312)696-4400 Fax: (312)318-0523
日本事務所：K

1, 7: シカゴの空の玄関オヘア空港につくられたエアーポート・ホテル。全室がスイート・ルームで構成されるマリオット・スイーツのひとつ。ひとつしかないレストラン「ウインドーズ」には、プライヴェート・ルームがあり、計100席。飾り気のない代表的なアメリカ料理のレストラン。2: シェフは、エルミニア・コタ女史。女性シェフはアメリカのホテルでは珍しくない。3: チーズ・バーガー、オニオン・リング添え。4: 鶏肉のグリル・サラダ。「チャイナ・タウン」と命名されている。5: メロンとスイカのデザート。6: アイス・ティー、セロリ添え。8: 内装にはエッチング・ガラスが使われている。

1, 7: This airport hotel, located at Chicago's O'Hare International Airport, is comprised entirely of suites. *Windows*, the only restaurant, seats 100 and has a separate private room. Straightforward, modern American cuisine is served. 2: Ms. Herminia Cota is the chef. 3: Cheeseburger with crisp onion rings. 4: "Chinatown" grilled duck salad. 5: A melon and watermelon dessert. 6: Iced tea with celery. 8: Etched glass panels decorate the interior.

1

2

PALMER'S STEAK & SEAFOOD HOUSE
The Palmer House & Towers
—A Hilton Hotel
17 East Monroe Street,
Chicago, Illinois 60603 U.S.A.
Tel:(321)726-7500 Fax:(321)917-1735
Telex:382182
日本事務所：G

1：レストラン・マネージャーのティモシー・フライト（写真:左）とレストラン・シェフのマーク・リプスコーム。1900年代初頭、このレストランはアルコール類のみを販売する男性専用のパブだった。**2**：シカゴのダウン・タウンに1871年に開業した初期グランド・ホテルのひとつ。**3,4**：レストラン「パーマーズ・ステーキ・アンド・シーフード・ハウス」は、シカゴ屈指のステーキ・ハウス。アメリカでも特に牛肉を大量消費するシカゴのシンボル的存在。アメリカン・ステーキの他、60品目を用意したサラダ・バー、輸入もののドーバー・ソール、マスなどが用意されている。

●●●

1: Restaurant manager Timothy Flight (left) and chef Mark Lipscomb. At the beginning of the 1900's this was a men's pub serving only alcoholic beverages. **2**: This early-period "Grand Hotel" first opened in 1871 in downtown Chicago. **3, 4**: Chicago is known for the quality and quantity of its beef, and *Palmer's Steak & Seafood House* is one of Chicago's leading steakhouses. In addition to American steak, the menu also features such items as trout, imported Dover sole, and a large salad bar with 60 items.

3

4

CAPE COD ROOM
The Drake
—A Vista International Hotel
Lake Shore Drive,
Chicago, Illinois 60611 U.S.A.
Tel:(312)787-2200 Fax:(312)787-1431
Telex:270278
日本事務所：G

1,2：1933年開店のレストラン「ケープ・コッド・ルーム」138席は、帆船内部を模した開店当時からの内装を今も保ち、数多くの受賞を誇るアメリカでもトップ・クラスのシーフード・レストラン。「オイスター・バー」9席を付帯。「レッド・スナッパー・スープ」、「メリイランド・クラブケーキ」などがおすすめ料理。大西洋・太平洋からの新鮮な魚介類が供される。
3：シカゴ、ミシガン湖畔に建つホテル。開業は1920年。

1, 2: The *Cape Cod Room* opened for business in 1933, and is decorated to resemble the interior of a luxury passenger ship. It has a reputation as one of the top-class seafood restaurants in America, and has won a number of awards. The seating capacity is 138, and the attached *Oyster Bar* seats nine. Fresh fish and seafood from both the Atlantic and Pacific are served; especially recommended are the red snapper soup and the Maryland crab cakes. 3: This hotel opened in 1920 on the shores of Chicago's Lake Michigan.

FOUNTAIN
Four Seasons Hotel Philadelphia
One Logan Square,
Philadelphia, Pennsylvania 19103 U.S.A.
Tel:(215)963-1500 Fax:(215)963-9562
Telex:00-831805
日本事務所：C

1： かつてアメリカ第2番目の首都だったフィラデルフィアのラクシャリー・ホテルで、開業は1983年。
2,3： イタリア、フランス、アメリカ料理を提供する「ファウンテン・レストラン」は、低カロリー、低コレステロール、減塩などのヘルシー料理も用意している。アペタイザーとメイン・ディッシュのあいだに、"口なおし"のシャーベットが出たり、サービスするスタッフと皿を下げるスタッフを区別するなど、最高のサービスが受けられる。

●●●

1: Philadelphia was America's second capital city; this luxury hotel opened here in 1983. 2, 3: *Fountain* restaurant serves Italian, French and American cuisine. There is also a health-oriented menu serving low-calorie, low-cholesterol and low-salt dishes. A sherbet is served between the appetizers and the main course to refresh the palate. Service is top class, with separate staffs to serve the food and to clear the plates afterwards.

Appetizers

BROILED SCALLOPS with PESTO
and SUN-DRIED TOMATOES
5.75

*GULF SHRIMP with DILL MAYONNAISE
7.95

*STONE CRAB CLAWS with COUNTRY MUSTARD SAUCE
(In Season)
7.95
— OR —
As a Hot Entree with Drawn Butter
17.95

FRESH OYSTERS on the HALF SHELL
With shallot vinaigrette.
4.95

HERB BREADED OYSTERS
Pan fried and served with champagne butter sauce.
5.50

*FRESH SMOKED SHRIMP with
LIMED JAPANESE HORSERADISH SAUCE
7.25

SEAFOOD SAUSAGE with SORREL SAUCE
6.50

ANGEL HAIR PASTA with DUCK and
SNOW PEAS in GINGERED CREAM
5.25

Soups

WHITE CONCH CHOWDER
4.00

FOUR ONION SOUP
3.50

WILD MUSHROOM SOUP BAKED with BRIE CHEESE
4.95

Salads

CAESAR SALAD (For Two) 4.95 Per Person
Prepared tableside in the traditional manner.

WILTED SPINACH with
HOT BACON DRESSING
(For Two) 4.95 Per Person
Prepared tableside.

HENRY'S SALAD 3.75
Limestone, radicchio, fresh tomato,
gorgonzolla cheese and
vinaigrette dressing.

Herbs and Spices

DILL
A small dark seed of dill plant grown
in India; aromatic, slightly sharp
taste resembling caraway. Used in sauces,
salads, soups and spiced vinegar.

GARLIC
The strong smelling bulb of this plant
is made up of small sections called
cloves and used as seasonings in
meats and salads.

BAY LEAVES
The aromatic leaf of the laurel, dried
and used as a spice in pickling,
stews and sauces.

GINGER
A spice from palmate-shaped root from
Asia and East Indies; strong piquant flavor.
Used cracked in chutneys, preserves,
dried fruits, tea and ground in cakes,
cookies, breads and canned fruits.

MUSTARD
Used whole in salads, pickled meats and
fish; dry in meats, sauces, gravy,
salad dressings; prepared (blend with
other spices, salt, vinegar) in sauces and
as meat accompaniment.

NUTMEG
From the hard, aromatic seed of an
East Indian tree. Used in puddings and
baked goods.

PAPRIKA
A spice from dried, ripe red sweet peppers,
with a pleasant odor and mild sweet
flavor. Used in fish, shellfish, stews,
salad dressings.

PEPPER
A spice from dried small round berry
(peppercorn) of climbing tropical vines,
with aromatic penetrating odor
and pungent flavor.

SWEET BASIL
An herb from dried aromatic leaves and
stems of small annual plant grown in India
and along the Mediterranean; clove-like
flavor. Used in meat pies, stews,
soups and dressing.

TARRAGON
An herb with pungent aromatic anise-
flavored leaves of tarragon plant.
Used in vinegar, sauces, mustard,
salads and soups.

THYME
An herb with aromatic leaves and
stems of small garden perennial, with
slightly pungent odor. Used in stews, soups,
poultry stuffings and meat loaves.

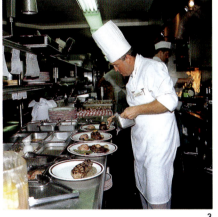

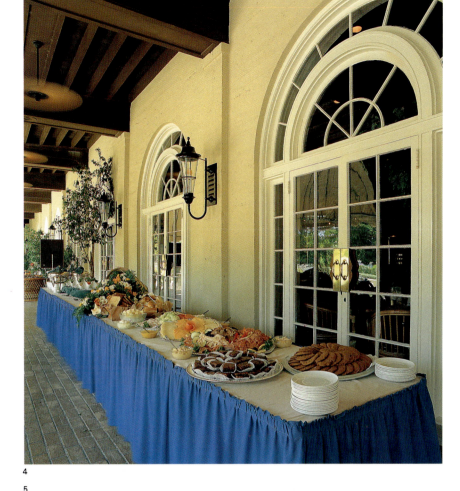

3

4

5

HENRY'S
Marriott's Casa Marina Resort
Peynolds Street on the ocean, Key West,
Florida 33040 U.S.A.
Tel:305-296-3535 Fax:ext. 7815
日本事務所：K

1：アメリカ最南端の島キー・ウエストに建てられた美しいリゾート・ホテルで、開業は1921年。2：料理に欠かせない多くのスパイスの花をデザインしたメニュー。3：キッチンで料理を仕上げるエグゼクティブ・スー・シェフのリチャード・ディングル。4, 5：マイアミ、キー・ウエスト間の鉄道を完成させ、ホテルの開業を前に他界した創業者ヘンリー・モリソン・フラッグラーにちなんで命名されたアメリカ料理のレストランである。日曜日にはレストラン外の広いヴェランダで"サンデー・ブランチ"が楽しめる。

●●●

1: This beautiful resort hotel opened in 1921 on the island of Key West at the southern tip of Florida. 2: The flowers of a number of spice plants decorate the menu. 3: Executive sous-chef Richard Dingle preparing food in the kitchen. American cuisine is the specialty here. 4, 5: *Henry's* restaurant is named after Henry Morrison Flagler, who built a railway line linking Miami with Key West. He was also the founder of the hotel, although he died before construction was completed. Sunday brunch is served on the wide veranda outside the restaurant.

WINDSOR
DINNING ROOM
Marriott's Castle
Harbour Resort
P.O.Box HM 841 Hamilton HMCX
Tucker's Town, Bermuda
Tel:809-293-2040 Fax:809-293-8288
Telex:3219 CASLE BA
日本事務所：K

1: テーブル・セッティング。朝食とコンチネンタル料理が提供される。2: レストランのスタッフ。3: レストランを預かるシェフたち。左よりガルド・マンジェ（肉担当）のシェフ、ダラン・ダンプラファイ、フード・プロダクションマネージャーのルイス・J・トロープ、アシスタント・ヘッド・ペストリー・シェフのアルフレッド・チョン。4: レストラン「ウインザー」ダイニング・ルームのメニュー。表紙はホテルの全景。5: 1931年開業のホテルを増改築し、1986年に再開業した大西洋の孤島バーミューダのリゾート・ホテル。6: バーミューダの代表的なスープであるバーミューダ・フィッシュ・チャウダー。7: 骨付き仔ヒツジ肉のハーブ味。ナス、トマト、ポテト、キノコが添えられる。8: サーモンのマスタード・ソース。

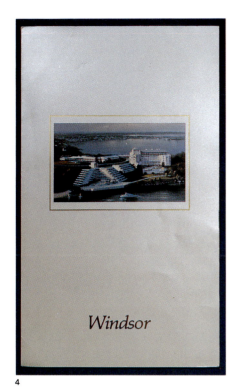
4

6

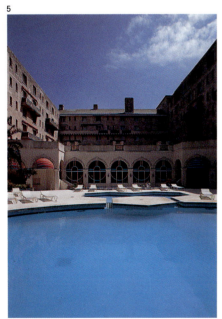
5

7

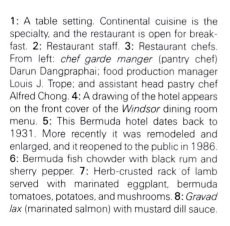

1: A table setting. Continental cuisine is the specialty, and the restaurant is open for breakfast. **2:** Restaurant staff. **3:** Restaurant chefs. From left: *chef garde manger* (pantry chef) Darun Dangpraphai; food production manager Louis J. Trope; and assistant head pastry chef Alfred Chong. **4:** A drawing of the hotel appears on the front cover of the *Windsor* dining room menu. **5:** This Bermuda hotel dates back to 1931. More recently it was remodeled and enlarged, and it reopened to the public in 1986. **6:** Bermuda fish chowder with black rum and sherry pepper. **7:** Herb-crusted rack of lamb served with marinated eggplant, bermuda tomatoes, potatoes, and mushrooms. **8:** *Gravad lax* (marinated salmon) with mustard dill sauce.

8

Great Hotels of the World: vol. 5 — 117

EL GOBERNADOR
Hotel Condado Beach
P.O.Box 4195, San Juan, Puerto Rico 00905
Tel:1809-721.60.90 Fax:1809-722.5062
Telex: 2433
日本事務所：B

1,2: スペイン料理のレストラン「エル・ゴベルナドール（総督）」ではショーが楽しめ、付帯する「バー」にはスペイン独特のタパスが用意されている。毎夜入口にシェフのおすすめ料理がディスプレイされる。
3: カリブ海の島プエリトリコのコンダード黄金海岸のリゾート・ホテル。開業は1919年。

1, 2: *El Gobernador* ("The Governor") serves Spanish cuisine and also presents a dinner show. Traditional Spanish *tapas* hors d'oeuvres are set out for patrons at the attached *Bar*, and the chef's recommended dishes of the day are on display each night at the restaurant entrance.
3: This resort hotel has been open since 1919 at Condado Beach on the Caribbean island of Puerto Rico.

1

2

FOUQUET'S DE PARIS
Camino Real D.F.
Mariano Escobedo 700
11590 Mexico, D.F.
Tel:(905)203-2121 Fax:(905)250-6897
日本事務所：Y

1：10ヵ所ある飲食施設のうちのメイン・ダイニング が、フランス美食料理の「フーケ・ド・パリ」。パリの シャンゼリゼにあるミシュラン一つ星(91年)の「フ ーケ」の直営店で、レストラン・バーも付いている。
2：海抜2,240メートルの首都メキシコ・シティー のチャプルテペック公園近くにあるメキシコを代表 するホテル。素晴らしい本場料理が楽しめる。

●●●●

1: *Fouquet's de Paris* serves as the hotel's main dining room, and is one of ten restaurants and lounges here. The restaurant specializes in gourmet French cuisine and includes a bar. It is under the direct management of *Fouquet's*, a Michelin one-star restaurant (1991) on the Champs Elysées in Paris. 2: Here, in this capital city 2,240 meters above sea level, this restaurant is highly regarded for its excellent food. This typical Mexican hotel is near the Bosque de Chapultepec public garden in Mexico City.

AZULEJOS
Camino Real Ixtapa
Playa Vista Hermosa, 40880,
Ixtapa/Zihuatanejo, Guerrero, Mexico
Tel:52-743-4-33-00 Fax:52-743-4-31-06
Telex:016-203
日本事務所：Y

1-5: メキシコ西海岸の保養地・イスタパに隣接するシワタネホ湾の美しいリゾート・ホテル。浜辺につづく傾斜地に建てられ、プライヴェート・ビーチを持っている。「アズレホス（陶タイル）」は、窓ガラスがまったくないオープン・エアーの珍しいレストランで、安定した気候がこの施設の開発を可能にした。床は陶タイル、ビュッフェ・テーブルは光沢タイルで装飾。レストランは写真：1の右上部に置かれている。

1-5: This beautiful resort hotel looks out over Zihuatanejo Bay, next to the resort of Ixtapa. The hotel extends down the sloping hillside leading to the shoreline, where guests can use the private beach. *Azulejos* ("glazed tiles") restaurant is features an unusual open-air plan, made possible by the mild climate. Glazed tiles cover the buffet table. (The restaurant can be seen in the upper right-hand of photo. no 1.

ASIA

アジア(ホンコン、ブルネイ、バンコック、シンガポール):味の万華鏡

　高温、多湿。東南アジアは自然から豊かな食材を得てきた。神への感謝から始まった祭りの名残りか、アジアの食事にはなんらかの儀式を伴っているものが多い。同じ皿から、箸で分ける……この単純なしきたりすら、もとは村の長がとりしきった原始共産社会の分配法だったという。箸はまた、アジア独特の繊細な味覚をはぐくんだ。いま、それぞれの民族料理が、食の世界を万華鏡のように彩っている。

　中国料理の原点であり、頂点でもあるといわれる満漢全席。かつて、漢の皇帝が中国全土から集めさせ、三日三晩かけて堪能したという美味・珍味の数々である。今日、これの再現料理をホンコンで味わうことができるが、最終日の晩餐の主役として供される龍(ヘビ)と虎(ネコ)のダイナミックな二品を見ると、食に対する人間の欲望と芸術というものを実感せずにいられない。(谷沢由起子)

Southeast Asia (Hong Kong, Brunei, Bangkok, Singapore): A Kaleidoscope of Flavors

With its warm temperatures and high humidity, southeast Asia offers a bounty of natural ingredients. Asian eating habits still reflect a number of practices that began with religious festivals and various ceremonies. For example, food is generally served in one large plate, then distributed to each person's individual plate with chopsticks. This simple custom goes back to the distant past—originally the village chief would distribute food to everyone, in an early manifestation of the communist social ideal of equal distribution of goods. The historic use of chopsticks also helped nurture some of the unique, subtle flavors found in Asian cuisines. Nowadays, the world of Asian food is a kaleidoscope of different traditional folk cuisines.

In ancient China the emperor would sometimes hold an "all-China feast," at which numerous delicacies and exotic flavors from throughout the country were assembled for an elaborate feast lasting three days and three nights. Today this cuisine is undergoing a revival in Hong Kong. Attending one of these banquets, and enjoying the main dish of the final night's feast—a dynamic presentation of dragon and tiger (actually snake and cat)—one cannot help but appreciate the combination of human artifice and appetite that merge together in the art of cooking. (Yukiko Tanizawa)

5

6

4

ONE HARBOUR ROAD
Grand Hyatt Hong Kong
1 Harbour Road, Hong Kong
Tel: 861-1234 Fax: 852-8611677
日本事務所：E

1, 2：ホテル前の道路と同名の「ワン・ハーバー・ロード」は広東料理のレストランで、196席。インテリア・デザインはハーシュ・ベドナー社。食器はリチャード・ジノリ焼。写真：1はレストラン上層部分。**3**：料理は左から、カニ爪のブイヨン、野菜炒め。ホタテと野菜の炒め四川風、中国ハム添え。奥がフカヒレのスープ、鳩の玉子添え、タケノコとキノコの炒めものが入っている。**4**：香港島のワンチャイ（湾仔）に1989年に開業したホテルで、575室。**5**：専用のエレヴェーターがロビーとレストラン下層を結ぶ。**6**：レストラン下層部分を上層から見る。**7**：シェフは中国本土から招聘している。

●●●

1, 2: *One Harbour Road* is a two-level Cantonese restaurant with seating for 196. It takes its name from the street address of the hotel. Servingware is by Richard Ginori. Hirsch Bedner was responsible for the interior design. Photo. no 1 shows the upper level. **3**: (From left): Baked crab claws in bouillon with sautéed vegetables; Szechwan-style sautéed scallops with ham and Chinese greens; (rear) shark's fin soup and braised bamboo and fungi with pigeon egg. **4**: This 575-room hotel opened in 1989 in Hong Kong Island's Wan Chai district. **5**: A non-stop elevator runs from the lobby to the restaurant's lower level. **6**: A view of the lower level from the upper level. **7**: The chef here was invited from the Chinese mainland.

7

GRISSINI
Grand Hyatt Hong Kong
1 Harbour Road, Hong Kong
Tel: 861-1234　Fax: 852-8611677
日本事務所：E

1：3階の北イタリア料理のレストラン「グリッシーニ」。グリッシーニとはイタリア独特の細い棒状のパンのこと。120席。レストラン・シェフはミラノ生まれのガブリエレ・コロンボ。2, 3：レストランの入口部分。4, 6：リチャード・ジノリ焼の食器とメニュー。5：入口に1,000本のワインを貯蔵するワイン・セラー。7：18人収容のプライヴェート・ルーム。8：レストラン・シェフのコロンボとドイツ生まれのエグゼクティブ・シェフのジョセフ・F・ブッディ（右）。シンガポール、バンコック、ケルンのハイアット・リージェンシー・ホテルのエグゼクティブ・シェフを経て現職。9：ハム、チーズ、サラダ、小エビなどをセットしたアンティパスト（オードブル）。10：レッド・スナッパー。11：カスタード・クリームのスポンジ・ケーキ。

●●●

1: *Grissini* restaurant occupies three levels and seats 120. The specialty is northern Italian cuisine, and the name comes from the word for a type of long, thin Italian bread. The chef, Gabriele Colombo, was born in Milan. 2, 3: The restaurant entrance area. 4, 6: Serviceware by Richard Ginori; a menu. 5: Near the entrance to the dining room is a wine cellar stocked with some 1,000 bottles. 7: A private room with seating for 18. 8: Chef Colombo (left) and executive chef Josef F. Budde. Budde was born in Germany, and has worked as executive chef at Hyatt Regency hotels in Singapore, Bangkok and Cologne, Germany. 9: Assorted hors d'oeuvres (*antipasto misto*), including ham, cheese, shrimps and salad. 10: Red snapper with bell peppers, potatoes and black olives (*dentice al forno con peperoni, patete e olive nere*). 11: Custard cream and sponge cake (*zuppa Inglese*).

GRAND CAFE
Grand Hyatt Hong Kong
1 Harbour Road, Hong Kong
Tel: 861-1234 Fax: 852-8611677
日本事務所：E

1：カジュアル・レストラン「グランド・カフェ」は九龍の夜景を一望できる人気スポット。2,4：黒御影石の円柱で飾られたダイニング・スペースは2つのエリアに分けられ、スープ、サラダ、サンドイッチ、ステーキなどのほか、オリエンタル料理が楽しめる。3：イタリアン・ケーキのティラミス、黒胡椒入りの丸チョコレートが人気。持ち帰り用の美しい創作ケーキを販売するコーナーが話題になっている。

1: The *Grand Cafe* is a casual restaurant popular for its nighttime view of Kowloon. 2, 4: Black granite columns decorate the interior, which is divided into two separate dining areas. In addition to soups, salads, sandwiches and steaks, Oriental dishes are also available. 3: Italian *tiramisù* cake and round chocolates with black pepper are popular items. Beautifully decorated cakes are available "to go" from the take-out area.

3

4

SUMMER PALACE
Island Shangri-La Hong Kong
Pacific Place, 88 Queensway, Central,
Hong Kong
Tel: 877-3838 Fax: 521-8742
Telex: 70373 ISLPP HX
日本事務所：S

1: 左から、タケノコの蒸し煮、鳩の玉子とブロッコリー添え。中央が、アワビの蒸し煮と中国野菜、オイスター・ソース。右が、ホタテのカニ玉子、中国ハムが使われている。奥が、カニ爪が入ったフカヒレ・スープ。2: 香港島のパシフィック・プレイス（ショッピング・コンプレックス）に1991年開業した高層ホテル。3: シェフはリー・カン。ラマダ・ルネサンス・ホテル・ホンコンに2年、レストラン「福臨門」で5年間働いてきた。4,5: 広東料理レストラン「サマー・パレス」は北京の"夏宮"をイメージした内装で、食器は日本製ナルミ。

1: (Left) braised bamboo shoots with pigeon eggs and broccoli; (center) braised abalone and Chinese vegetables with oyster sauce; (right) steamed scallops with crabmeat and garden vegetables; (back) braised shark's fin soup with crab claws. 2: This high-rise hotel opened in 1991 in the Pacific Place shopping complex on Hong Kong Island. 3: Chef Lee Keung worked two years at the Ramada Renaissance Hotel Hong Kong and five years at *Fook Lam Moon* restaurant before coming here. 4, 5: A "Peking Palace" theme was the inspiration for the *Summer Palace* Cantonese restaurant's interior. Servingware is Narumi china from Japan.

4

5

NADAMAN
Island Shangri-La Hong Kong
Orange Grove Road, Singapore 1025
Tel: 737-3644 Fax: 733-7220, 1029
Telex: RS 21505
日本事務所：S

1：160年の歴史を持つ正統日本料理の老舗「なだ万」の香港2号店で、1991年春に開店。写真はレストラン部分。中央奥に寿司カウンター。ほかに3室の畳の間、鉄板焼コーナーがある。2：左下は、3種類の「先付け」、「酢の物」、「前菜」、冷し素麺の「食事」。中央が、キーウィー・フルーツとスイカのジュースの「箸洗い替り」、「煮物」、神戸牛冷しシャブの「合い肴」。右が「吸物」と「焼物」、右上が「造り」と抹茶ティラミス・アズキ添えの「デザート」。涼しさを感じさせる夏の懐石献立。3：料理長の大嶋高幸とマネージャーの藤原康隆。4：スタッフの衣装も着物で統一。

1: *Nadaman*, which opened in the spring of 1991, is the second Hong Kong branch of a traditional Japanese restaurant with a distinguished 160-year history. The photo shows part of the restaurant. To the center rear is a sushi bar. There are also three tatami mat rooms and a teppanyaki area. 2: (From lower left) appetizer, vinegared dish, hors d'oeuvre, cold *somen* noodles; (center) a refreshment made from kiwi fruit and watermelon, a cold Kobe beef dish; (right) soup, broiled dish; (upper right) fresh raw fish, a dessert of green tea *tira-misù* cake with azuki beans. This summer *kaiseki* meal is filled with cool, refreshing flavors. 3: Head chef Takayuki Oshima and manager Steve Fujiwara. 4: The staff wear traditional kimonos.

1
2

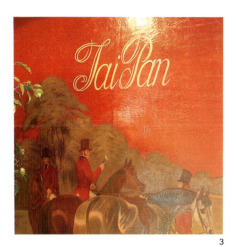

TAI PAN
Omni The Hongkong Hotel
Harbour City, Kowloon, Hong Kong
Tel: 736-0088 Fax: 736-0011
日本事務所：X

1：コンチネンタル料理の「タイパン」レストランは60席。2：エグゼクティブ・シェフ（中央）はオーストリア生れのピーター・カセラー。バーミューダ、デトロイトのホテル、マンダリン・ジャカルタ、ザ・オリエンタル・バンコックなどを経て現職。料理は左から、スモーク・サーモンとカニのミルフイユ、野菜添え。右が、茹でたカレイとロブスターのメダリオン、ライト・シャンパン・ソース。奥が、砂糖でつくった籠をディスプレイしたラズベリーのムース、マンゴー・ソース。季節のフルーツが添えられる。3，4：昼はビュッフェ形式のアペタイザーが楽しめる。また、このレストランは接続する駐車場（6階）からの専用入口を持つ。5：九龍のスター・フェリー乗場に隣接する18階建のホテル。開業は1969年11月。ヴィクトリア・ハーバーを一望するウォーター・フロントに位置している。

●●●

1: *Tai Pan* restaurant serves Continental cuisine and seats 60. 2: Executive chef Peter Kaserer (center) was born in Austria and worked at hotels in Bermuda and Detroit as well as the Mandarin Jakarta and The Oriental, Bangkok, before coming here. (Left) Mille-feuille of smoked salmon and snow crab with fresh vegetables; (right) poached brill and lobster medallions served in a light champagne sauce; (back) light raspberry mousseline in a sugar basket with mango sauce and a variety of seasonal fruits. 3, 4: A buffet-style appetizer table is offered at lunchtime. The restaurant has its own entrance from the connecting sixth-floor parking garage. 5: This Kowloon hotel stands on the Waterfront next to the Star Ferry terminal, and offers a sweeping view of Victoria Harbor. The 18-story hotel opened in November, 1969.

T'ANG COURT
**Ramada Renaissance Hotel
Hong Kong**

8 Peking Road, Tsimshatsui, Kowloon,
Hong Kong
Tel: 311-3311 Fax: 311-6611
日本事務所：Q

1:「タン・コート」は中国本土直送の中国茶がセレクトできる広東料理のレストラン。2: 九龍のチムシャツイ（尖沙阻）南に立つ19階建の近代ホテル。3: 昼食には20種類以上の特製ディン・サム（飲茶）が楽しめる。4: エグゼクティブ・シェフのホー・シイウ・ワー。広東生れで、30年のキャリアを持つ。香港の料理学校、リージェント香港、シンガポールのフラマ・ホテルなどを経て、90年から現職。

●●●

1: *T'ang Court* serves Cantonese cuisine and also offers a selection of Chinese teas imported directly from the mainland. 2: This modern 19-story hotel is at the south end of Tsim Sha Tsui in Kowloon, Hong Kong. 3: More than twenty varieties of *dim sum* are served at lunchtime. 4: Ho Siu Wah is the executive chef for Chinese cuisine. Born in Canton, he has a career spanning some thirty years. Before coming here in 1990 he worked at the Tak Shun Cooking School Hong Kong, the Regent Hong Kong, and the Furama Hotel, Singapore.

3

4

MAN WAH
Mandarin Oriental, Hong Kong
5 Connaught Road, Central, Hong Kong
Tel: 522-0111 Fax: 810-6190 Telex: 73653
日本事務所：L

1：ヘッド・シェフは3年勤続のライ・カン・ルン。2：最上階にあるのが、高い評価を受けているクラシック・スタイルの広東料理のレストラン「マン・ワ」。3：香港島セントラル地区に1963年開業のホテル。4：蒸したホタテ包みとカニ爪。5：冬メロンで巻いた細切りのロースト・ダック、ユナン・ハム、黒マッシュルーム、中国野菜添え。6：シタビラメのフィレのソテーにブラック・ビーンズ・ソース。デコレーションにはニンジンでつくられた"龍"や"白鳥"が使われる。

●●●

1: Head chef Lai Kam Lun has been here three years. 2: *Man Wah* is on the top floor and serves classic Cantonese cuisine. The restaurant has maintained a long-standing reputation for the excellent quality of its food. The interior is filled with Chinese-style rosewood furnishings, and there is a separate private dining room seating 12. 3: This hotel has been in business since 1963 in Hong Kong Island's Central District. 4: Steamed diced scallops wrapped in egg white and accompanied by sautéed fresh crab claws. 5: Steamed sliced roast duck, Yunnan ham and black mushrooms wrapped in winter melon and served with Chinese vegetables. 6: Sautéed fillet of sole with green vegetables in black bean sauce. Decorating the dish are swans, dragons, and other animals from Chinese legends, carved from carrots.

Great Hotels of the World: vol. 5 — 141

PIERROT
Mandarin Oriental, Hong Kong
5 Connaught Road, Central, Hong Kong
Tel: 522-0111 Fax: 810-6190 Telex: 73653
日本事務所：L

1, 3, 4: 九龍市街を見渡すホテル最上階にあるクラシック・スタイルのフランス料理レストラン「ピエロ」。バー「ハーレクイン」を付帯する。カエデ材の壁パネルで装飾したインテリアはドン・アシュトンのデザイン。食器は特注の日本製ナルミ。中華料理レストラン「マン・ワ」と同様、他の客への配慮から12歳以下の子供は入場できない。**2:** エグゼクティブ・シェフはスイス生れのユルク・ミュンヒ。チューリッヒのレストランを振出しに、1980年から香港のザ・エクセルシオール、ザ・オリエンタル・マカオを経て、1987年より当ホテルに勤務。**5:** ウェールズ産仔ヒツジのカルパッチョ・トリュフ・オイル、アスパラガスのムース添え。**6:** 蒸したイシナギのフィレ、カレー・バター・ソース。**7:** ケシのケーキとアーモンド・アイスクリーム、フルーツ添え。

●●●

1, 3, 4: *Pierrot* restaurant serves classic-style French cuisine and also has an attached bar, *Harlequin*. From its top-floor location it offers panoramic views of Hong Kong's Kowloon peninsula. Don Ashton was responsible for the interior design, which features maplewood-paneled walls. The servingware is specially made Narumi china from Japan. Out of consideration for their patrons, this restaurant and the Chinese restaurant *Man Wah* do not allow children under the age of twelve. **2:** Jürg Münch is the executive chef. After starting out at *Chez Max* in Zurich, since 1980 Chef Münch has worked at The Excelsior Hotel in Hong Kong and The Oriental in Macao. He came here in 1987. **5:** Carpaccio of Welsh lamb with green asparagus mousse and truffle oil (*carpaccio d'agneau aux asperges*). **6:** Steamed fillet of sea bass in a light curry butter (*Vapeur de loup de mer au beurre de curry*). **7:** Poppyseed cake and almond ice cream (*gâteau de pavot et crème glacée aux amandes*).

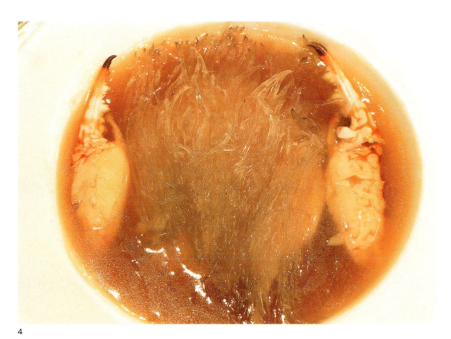

4

3

MAN HO
Hong Kong Marriott
Pacific Place, 88 Queensway, Hong Kong
Tel:810-8366 Fax:845-0737
日本事務所：K

1：3階にあるクラシック・スタイルの広東料理のレストラン「マン・ホー」。エグゼクティブ・シェフはサイモン・チュイ。2：7種のフカヒレ・スープ、6種のツバメの巣料理が用意され、昼食にはディン・サム（飲茶）も楽しめる。メニュー。3：香港島パシフィック・プレイスに立つアメリカ・ホテル産業の雄マリオット社のアジア進出第1号ホテル。開業は1989年2月。4：フカヒレ・スープ、カニ爪添え。5：ホタテのソテー・四川風、くるみ添え。6：ゴマのパンケーキ。

●●●

1: The third-floor Chinese restaurant *Man Ho* specializes in classic-style Cantonese cuisine. Simon Chui is the executive chef. 2: The menu offers seven different types of shark's fin soup and six different bird's nest dishes, as well as a variety of *dim sum* items at lunchtime. 3: Open in February, 1989, this is the first Asian hotel developed by Marriott Corporation, America's leading hotel company. It is part of Hong Kong Island's Pacific Place complex. 4: Shark's fin soup with walnuts. 5: Szechwan-style sautéed scallops with walnuts. 6: Pan-fried sesame pancakes.

5

6

Great Hotels of the World: vol. 5 ——— 145

J.W.'S GRILL
Hong Kong Marriott
Pacific Place, 88 Queensway, Hong Kong
Tel: 810-8366　Fax: 845-0737
日本事務所：K

1, 2: マリオット社の創業者ジョン・ウィラード・マリオットの名を冠したメイン・ダイニング。マホガニーの壁材とワイン・カラーの大理石で装飾され、ロブスター、シーフード、アメリカ牛などを提供。夜はピアノの生演奏がある。入口に同名の「バー」を付帯する。3: 香港島パシフィック・プレイスに建てられた3つのホテル。左からホンコン・マリオット、コンラッド・ホンコン、そしてアイランド・シャングリラ。

1, 2: *J. W.'s Grill* takes its name from the initials of John Willard Marriott, the founder of the hotel chain. The interior features mahogany walls and wine-colored marble, and there is a bar at the entrance. Lobster, seafood and American beef are served. In the evenings diners can enjoy live piano music performances. 3: Hong Kong Island's Pacific Place includes three hotels: (from left) Hong Kong Marriott Hotel; Hotel Conrad Hong Kong; and Island Shangri-La.

1

NICHOLINI'S
Hotel Conrad Hong Kong
Pacific Place, 88 Queensway, Hong Kong
Tel: 521-3838 Fax: 521-3888
日本事務所：F

1：アメリカで247のホテルを運営するヒルトン・ホテルズ・コーポレーションのアジア進出第1号店。香港島のパシフィック・プレイスに1990年6月開業。8階にある北イタリア料理レストラン「ニコリーニズ」は、入口をムラノ・ガラスで飾り、カラフルな色調で内装をコーディネート。2, 3：食器は日本製のナルミで、手書き絵付けの特注品。グラスはイタリア製のスカーヴォ。

1: This is the first Asian hotel run by the Hilton Hotels Corporation, which manages 247 hotels in America. Part of the Pacific Place complex on Hong Kong Island, it opened in June 1990.
 Nicholini's restaurant, on the eighth floor, serves northern Italian cuisine. The interior is particularly colorful, and the entrance area is decorated with Murano glass. 2, 3: The specially made Narumi china from Japan features a hand-painted design. The glassware is Italian Scavo glass.

2

3

1

2

GOLDEN LEAF RESTAURANT
Hotel Conrad Hong Kong
Pacific Place, 88 Queensway, Hong Kong
Tel: 521-3838 Fax: 521-3888
日本事務所：F

1：ホテル・コンラッド・ホンコンの広東料理の小レストラン「ゴールデン・リーフ」。3つのプライヴェート・ダイニング・ルームがある。椅子はファ・リ・ローズウッド・チェアーと呼ばれる中国独特のもの。壁には中国四大王朝の風景を描いたスクリーン・パネルが4枚飾られている。2：レストラン・マネージャーのエドモンド・チャン。マスター・シェフはラム・シン・ロン。3,4：黒と金の格子デザインのナルミ食器と象牙の箸。

1: *Golden Leaf* is a small Cantonese restaurant in the Hotel Conrad Hong Kong. The restaurant includes three private dining rooms, and it is furnished with unique Chinese *fa li* rosewood chairs. On the wall are four screen panels with Chinese dynasty-style landscapes. 2: Restaurant manager Edmond Chan and master Chinese chef Lam Sing Lun. 3, 4: The servingware is black and gold lattice pattern Narumi china, and the chopsticks are ivory.

3

4

3

4

GADDI'S
The Peninsula, Hong Kong
Salisbury Road, Kowloon, Hong Kong
Tel:366-6251 Fax:722-4170 Telex:43821
日本事務所：P

1: 第二次世界大戦後長年支配人を勤めたレオ・ガッディにちなんで命名されたフランス料理のレストラン「ガッディーズ」。クリストフルのシャンデリア、ドイツ製の食器ローゼンタールが使われている。**2**: メニュー。**3**: エグゼクティブ・シェフはエリック・シェーリ。**4**: 仔ヒツジのノワゼット・唐辛子、チーズ・ラヴィオリ添え。**5**:「ガッディーズの太鼓」と名付けられた特製デザート。シャーベットとフルーツが使われ、砂糖でつくった籠が添えられる。**6**: 1928年に開業した香港のランド・マーク・ホテル。

●●●

1: *Gaddi's* restaurant serves French cuisine. It is named after Leo Gaddi, who was the hotel's general manager for many years after World War II. The crystal chandelier here is by Christofle of Paris, and the servingware is made in Germany by Rosenthall. **2**: The restaurant menu. **3**: Executive chef Erich Schaeli. **4**: Lamb noisettes with capsicum and fresh cheese ravioli. **5**: "Timbale Gaddi's," a special dessert made with sherbet and fruit and garnished with a basket made from sugar. **6**: This landmark hotel has served visitors to Hong Kong since 1928.

5

6

4

3

LAI CHING HEEN
The Regent Hong Kong
Salisbury Road, Kowloon, Hong Kong
Tel: 721-1211 Fax: 739-4546 Telex: HX37134
日本事務所：R

1：スー・シェフのチャン・ヤン・タとヘッド・ウェイターのヨン・ワイ・チャーン。2：テーブル上のプレゼンテーション・プレートとナプキン・リングは手彫りの翡翠。箸は象牙を銀で装飾。3：九龍のウォーター・フロントに1980年10月開業した近代的ホテル。広東料理レストラン「ライ・チン・ヒーン」から香港島とヴィクトリア・ハーバーを一望できる。134席。4：エビ、ハム、ピーマンの炒め。5：レタスに盛られたヤリイカ、サヤエンドウの賽の目きざみ炒め・チリソース。6：昼食に提供される飲茶を準備するキッチン。

●●●

1: Sous-chef Chan Yan Tak and headwaiter Yeung Wai Cheung. 2: The service plates and napkin holders are handmade from green jade. The ivory chopsticks are decorated with silver. 3: This modern hotel opened in October 1980 on the Kowloon waterfront. *Lai Ching Heen* Cantonese restaurant offers a splendid view of Victoria Harbour, and seats 134. 4: Sautéed fresh prawns and ham with bell peppers. 5: Sautéed minced squid and string beans in chili sauce wrapped in lettuce. 6: The Kitchen, where lunchtime *dim sum* is being prepared.

5

6

THE HERITAGE
Sheraton Urama Hotel
Jalan Bendahara 2087 Bandar Seri Begawan,
Negara Brunei Darussalam
Tel:(673)(2)44272 Fax:(673)(2)21579
日本事務所：T

1：回教徒のスルタンが治める国にふさわしく、レストランの名も「ヘリテージ（世襲財産）」。歴代のスルタンの写真が壁を飾り、伝統的なフランス料理を提供する。2：世界一豊かな国ともいわれる産油国ブルネイの首都バンダル・セリ・ベガワンのホテル。3, 4：昼食も提供する「プールサイド・テラス」。左からセールス部長のV・マクリーン女史、エグゼクティブ・シェフのP・R・ノヴェラズ、総支配人のP・アラトサス。カレー料理、マレー料理が専門で、串刺しの肉料理（サテー）がおすすめ。カジュアル・レストランの「カフェ・メラティ」ではビュッフェも用意されている。

●●●

1: *Heritage* is perhaps an appropriate name for this traditional French restaurant in this traditional Islamic sultanate. Photographs of sultans from the past line the wall. 2: The oil-producing nation of Brunei Darussalam is often said to be the richest country in the world. This hotel serves the capital city of Bandar Seri Begawan. 3, 4: The *Poolside Terrace* also serves lunch. From left are Vicky Mclean, director of sales; Pascal R. Noverraz, executive chef; and Peter Alatsas, general manager. Curry dishes and Malay cuisine are served, and the skewered meat satays are especially recommended. *Cafe Melati* has a casual atmosphere and offers buffet-style service.

2

SHANG PALACE
Shangri-La Hotel Singapore
Orange Grove Road, Singapore 1025
Tel: 737-3644 Fax: 733-7220, 1029
Telex: RS 21505
日本事務所：S

1,2: 3棟のなかのメイン・ビルディング（旧館）1階に設けられた中華料理レストラン。現在ではむしろ珍しいものになった中国式装飾の内装。多種多様な中華料理を提供し、昼食には100品目もの飲茶が用意される。シンガポールを代表する中華レストラン。3: プライヴェート・ルームも数室ある。4: J・ヒルトンの小説"失なわれた地平線"に登場する架空の理想郷シャングリラから名を取ったシンガポールの庭園ホテル。1971年の開業。

1, 2: The hotel contains three separate wings; *Shang Palace* Chinese restaurant is on the first floor of the main building. The interior is decorated in traditional Chinese style, and the menu offers a wide range of Chinese dishes, including more than 100 *dim sum* dishes at lunchtime. The restaurant has a reputation for serving some of Singapore's finest Chinese food. 3: A number of private rooms are also available. 4: This Singapore "garden hotel" opened in 1971. The name Shangri-La is taken from the fictional paradise of James Hilton's 1933 novel, *Lost Horizon*.

3

4

1

2

NADAMAN
Shangri-La Hotel Singapore
Orange Grove Road, Singapore 1025
Tel: 737-3644 Fax: 733-7220, 1029
Telex: RS 21505
日本事務所：S

1-3：メイン・ビルディングの最上階にある日本料理の「なだ万」。1830年（天保元年）、初代・灘屋万助が、大阪で開店した老舗「なだ万」のシンガポール店。四季おりおりの伝統的な日本料理が楽しめ、寿司カウンター、鉄板焼コーナー、ダイニング・ルーム、畳の間が用意されている。1：鉄板焼のチーフ・シェフは宮迫征弘（みやさこ・ゆきひろ）。現在は、香港のアイランド・シャングリラに赴任。

●●●

1-3: *Nadaman* Japanese restaurant is on the top floor of the main building of the hotel here. It is the Singapore branch of a famous old restaurant established in Osaka in 1830 by Nadaya Mansuke. The specialty is traditional, orthodox Japanese cuisine reflecting the changing seasons. The restaurant includes a sushi bar, teppanyaki area, dining room and tatami mat area. 1: Head teppanyaki chef Miyasako Yukihiro has since moved to the Island Shangri-La in Hong Kong.

3

HOUSE OF BLOSSOMS
Marina Mandarin Singapore
6 Raffles Boulevard #01-100,
Marina Square Singapore 0103
Tel:338-3388 Fax:339-4977
日本事務所：V

1,2：潮州料理、広東料理のレストラン「ハウス・オブ・ブロッサムズ」。昼食には飲茶も用意されている。128席。3：地下のショッピング・コンプレックスが3つのホテルを結ぶシンガポールの新しいホテル都市マリーナ・スクエァーに、アメリカの建築家ジョン・ポートマンの設計で1987年1月開業したマリーナ・マンダリン・シンガポール。16階分を吹き抜いたアトリウムのある577室の大ホテル。

●●●

1,2: *House of Bloossoms* specializes in Teochew and Cantonese cuisines, and serves *dim sum* at lunchtime. The restaurant seats 128. **3:** Marina Square is Singapore's new "hotel city," with three hotels connected to an underground shopping complex. It was designed and built by American real estate developer John Portman. Marina Mandarin Singapore opened here in January 1987. It includes 577 guest rooms and a gigantic, 16-story atrium.

1

2

BOLOGNA
Marina Mandarin Singapore
6 Raffles Boulevard #01-100,
Marina Square Singapore 0103
Tel: 338-3388 Fax: 339-4977
日本事務所：V

1.2： 3ヵ所のレストランのうち、メイン・ダイニングのイタリア料理レストラン「ボローニャ」。132席。中世後期にヨーロッパの学問と食文化をリードしたボローニャにちなんで命名。カラーラ産大理石の床、ルネサンス調の絵画で飾られ、昼食にはイタリアの伝統的アンティパスト（オードブル）・ビュッフェが楽しめる。

●●●

1, 2: *Bologna*, one of the hotel's three restaurants, serves as the main dining room. It offers Italian cuisine and seats 132. The restaurant is named after the city of Bologna, an independent city-state and center of learning and culture during the Middle Ages. The floors are covered in Carrara marble, while Renaissance-style paintings line the walls. Lunchtime patrons can help themselves from a sumptuous buffet table laden with traditional Italian antipasto hors d'oeuvres.

TIKI
Pan Pacific Singapore
Marina Square, 7 Raffles Boulevard
Singapore 0103
Tel: 336-8111　Fax: 339-1861
日本事務所：0

1,2: パン・パシフィック・シンガポールは37階、800室の超高層ホテルで、1986年11月の開業。9ヵ所の飲食施設がある。「ティキ」はポリネシア料理を提供するエスニック・レストランで、南太平洋文化圏独特の彫像(ティキ)や竹林を巧みにあしらった内装が印象的。138席。3: 写真左からザ・オリエンタル・シンガポール、マリーナ・マンダリン・シンガポール、パン・パシフィック・シンガポール。

1,2: Pan Pacific Singapore has been open since November 1986. The 37-story, high-rise hotel has 800 guest rooms and nine restaurants and bars. *Tiki* restaurant serves Polynesian cuisine. The exotic interior incorporates a bamboo grove and several large South Pacific tiki statues, and seats 138. 3: From left: The Oriental, Singapore; Marina Mandarin Singapore; and Pan Pacific Singapore hotels.

1

2

HAI TIEN LO
Pan Pacific Singapore
Marina Square, 7 Raffles Boulevard
Singapore 0103
Tel:336-8111 Fax:339-1861
日本事務所：0

1,2：三角形のホテル・ビルの頂部、37階に張り出した円形部分が広東料理レストランの「ハイ・テン・ロー（海天楼）」。170席。外壁に設置されたシースルー・エレヴェーターがレストランに直結し、晴れた日にはマレーシアやインドネシアの島々まで、大パノラマが眺望できる。飲茶も用意され、プライヴェート・ルームも数ヵ所設けられている。

1, 2: *Hai Tien Lo* restaurant occupies part of the circular balcony projecting from the 37th floor of this triangle-shaped tower. The restaurant serves Cantonese cuisine and seats 170. Glass-walled elevators on the outside of the building provide direct access to the restaurant. On clear days, diners can enjoy a remarkable panoramic view extending as far as Malaysia and the Indonesian islands. *Dim sum* is also served, and the restaurant provides a number of private dining rooms.

COMPASS ROSE
The Westin Stamford & Plaza
2, Stamford Road, Singapore 0617
Tel: 338-8585 Fax: 338-2862
日本事務所：Y

1-3: 1986年7月に開業したウエスティン・スタンフォードは72階建の超高層ホテル・ビル。頂部（69〜71階）のレストラン「コンパス・ローズ」は、ロビーと専用の高速エレヴェーターで直結され、シンガポール随一のパノラマを誇る。244席。インターナショナル料理を提供し、同名のバーを付帯する。**4**: ラッフルズ・シティは、3万1千㎡の敷地に開発されたシンガポールの複合機能都市。ウエスティン・スタンフォード（1,253室）とプラザ（796室）のツイン・ホテル、コンヴェンション・センター、72店舗のブティック、オフィス・ビルから構成される。

●●●

1-3: *Compass Rose* spans the top three floors (69 through 71) of The Westin Stamford, which opened in July 1986. A high-speed elevator provides direct service from the lobby. The 244-seat restaurant specializes in international cuisine and also includes a bar. It is probably best known, though, for its incredible panoramic view. And with its height of 72 stories, The Westin Stamford is almost certainly the tallest hotel in the world. **4**: Raffles City is a newly developed multi-purpose complex stretching over 7.6 acres (330,000 square feet). It includes twin hotels—The Westin Stamford (with 1,253 rooms), and Plaza (with 796 rooms)—as well as a convention center, 72 boutiques and an office building.

LI-BAI
Sheraton Towers Singapore
39, Scotts Road, Singapore 0922
Tel: 737-6888 Fax: 737-1072
日本事務所：T

1, 2, 4: 広東料理のレストラン「リ・バイ（李白）」は、入口部分の大窓からロビーの吹き抜けを見渡す開放的な設計。プレゼンテーション・プレートはレストランの名を刻んだ翡翠の特注品。箸は象牙。おすすめ料理は、フカヒレの形を崩さず煮込んだフカヒレ・スープ。**3:** 特別なサービスを提供する部屋を設けるというシェラトン社のコンセプト"タワーズ"のアイディアにもとづき、410全室がバトラーのサービスが受けられる。開業は1985年12月。

●●●

1, 2, 4: The airy, open plan of *Li-Bai* Cantonese restaurant includes a large window at the entrance area offering a clear view of the lobby. The restaurant name is inscribed on the green jade service plates. The chopsticks are made from ivory. The shark's fin soup is highly recommended. The soup is prepared in an unusual style in which the original shape of the shark's fin is retained. **3:** This Singapore hotel opened in December 1985 and is known for its excellent level of service. The idea for the hotel originally developed from the special high-level "Towers" class of service offered to guests staying on certain floors of Sheraton hotels. Here, guests in all 410 rooms enjoy this deluxe treatment, which includes butler service.

NORMANDIE
The Oriental, Bangkok
48 Oriental Avenue, Bangkok 10500, Thailand
Tel: 2-236-1936 Fax: 2-236-1936
Telex: 82997 ORIENTAL TH
日本事務所：L

1,4：8つあるレストランのうち、メイン・ダイニングがフランス料理の「ノルマンディ」。チャオ・プラヤ川を望む中央棟最上部に位置している。2：エグゼクティブ・シェフはN.A.コストナー。スイスのル・モントルー・パレスなどを経て現職。3：世界最高のサービスを提供する3棟構成、394室の名門ホテル。5：リバー・サイドのオープン・エアー・レストラン「バーベキュー・ナイツ」から見た中央棟。

1,4: *Normandie*, specializing in French cuisine, is one of eight restaurants here and serves as the main dining room. Situated on the top floor of the central wing, it looks out over the Chao Phraya River. 2: Executive chef Norbert A. Kostner's past experience includes a stint at *Le Montreux Palace* in Switzerland. 3: This famous hotel is reputed to provide the best service in the world. There are three wings and 394 guest rooms. 5: A view of the central wing from the open-air riverside restaurant *Barbecue Nights*. *Normandie* is on the top floor.

4

5

AUSTRALIA

オーストラリア：野趣に富む巨大な島

アメリカより遅れて誕生した、もう一つの新大陸である。中央部にひろがる砂漠地帯を囲みながら、海岸沿いに緑濃いグリーン・ベルトが走る。国家としての若さを象徴するようなみずみずしい大自然が、いまや地球の財産になっている。開放的で温かい人情……の一方、アングロ・サクソンの伝統を引き継いで、環境保護の先端を行く。

もてなし料理というと、ビーフ、マトンといった尋常なものから、食用に養殖されたワニ、カンガルー、ワラビー（カンガルーより小型で、肉も柔らかい）、さらにラクダまで出る。長年グルメから珍重された海亀の料理は、いまではチャンスがない。養殖不可能な野生動物にたいして法はきびしいのだ。魚介類は潤沢で、この国でも地中海料理が人気上昇中。市場にはヘリや小型機に乗って買いつけに来る人も。乾いた空気に、地元のボルドー系のワインがおいしい。（谷沢由起子）

●●●

Australia: A Huge Island Rich in Nature

Founded even later than the United States of America, this is also a new country spreading out across a broad new continent. Stretching along the seacoast around the country is a wide, rich green belt which surrounds the huge desert region in the center. The fresh, wide-open countryside that symbolized the relative youthfulness of the country has now come to be regarded as one of the earth's important assets. The people of Australia express their feelings warmly, yet guard their heritage of Anglo-Saxon tradition. They also play a leading role in the preservation of the natural environment.

When Australians dine out or entertain at home, meat is a mainstay, ranging from the ordinary—beef and mutton—to the more unusual—farm-bred crocodile, kangaroo and wallaby (smaller in size than a kangaroo and with tenderer meat), and even camel. For many years sea turtle was highly prized by gourmets, but it is no longer available, and strict laws protect those wild animals that can't be raised on farms. Fish and seafood are available in many varieties, however, and because of this, Mediterranean cuisine is becoming more popular. At the marketplaces one can even find customers who have arrived by helicopter or light airplane to do their shopping. And when it comes to wine, the locally grown Bordeaux-derived wines benefit from the dry air and are very flavorful as a result. (Yukiko Tanizawa)

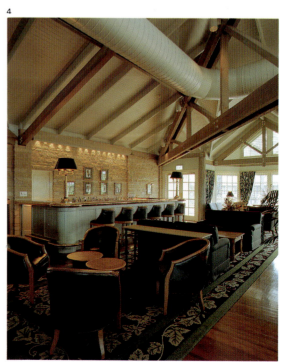

5

6

7

THE GRANGE
Hyatt Regency Sanctuary Cove
Hope Island, P.O.Box 2148
Southport, Queensland 4215, Australia
Tel:61-75-30-1234 Fax:61-75-578-234
Telex:140268
日本事務所：E

1,2：昼食には豊富なオードヴルとデザートのビュッフェが用意される。3：メニューとワイン・リスト。4：バーやプライヴェート・ルームもある。5：1988年6月開業した邸宅様式のホテル。6：地主屋敷の様式で離れとして建てられたレストラン「グレインジ」。7：左からマネージャーのJ・ブランスキル。シェフのE・ローゼンクランツ。料理は左から甲殻類のトリオ、サーロイン・ステーキ、マスとベイ・バック（甲殻類）のパイ。8：テーブル・セッティング。9：サウス・オーストラリア州の高級品を含め、多数のオーストラリア・ワインが用意されている。左からペンフォルズ・グレインジ・ハーミテイジ・1982、ペタルマ・クーナワラ・1985、リンデマンズ・クーナワラ・ピラス・1985。

●●●

1,2: Sumptuous hors d'oeuvre and dessert buffets are offered at lunchtime. 3: The menu and wine list. 4: The restaurant includes a bar and a private dining room. 5: This mansion-style hotel opened in June 1988. 6: *The Grange* restaurant occupies its own, provincial-style building. 7: From left: manager John Brunskill and chef Edwin Rosenkranz. Food (from left): trio of crustaceans with citrus butter sauce served with snowpeas and red pepper salad; grilled prime sirloin steak with button mushrooms and chipped potatoes; flan of coral trout and bugtails with salmon caviar and vermouth butter. 8: A table setting. 9: There is a wide selection of Australian wines available, including fine-quality wines from South Australia. Wines from left: Penfold's Grange Hermitage 1982; Petaluma Coonawarra 1985; Lindeman's Coonawarra Pyrus 1985.

8

9

HORIZONS
Sheraton Mirage Gold Coast
Seaworld Drive, Broadwater Spit, Main Beach,
Queensland 4217, Australia
Tel:075-91 1488 Fax:075-91 2299
Telex:AA41588/SHER GC
日本事務所：T

1：クィーンズランド料理のレストラン「ホライズンズ」。食器はヴィレロイ・アンド・ボッホ焼、デルタ・デザイン。輸入ワインも用意されている。2：シェフは、マルセロ・コステンベイダー。料理は左から、クィーンズランド産タイガー・プローン、唐辛子とライムのドレッシング。右が牛フィレのグリル。奥がパイナップルのカラメル・パイ、ラム・ソース。3：ゴールド・コースト北部の近代的リゾート・ホテル。1988年9月開業。

1: *Horizons* offers "Queensland cuisine" and a selection of imported wines. The servingware is Delta pattern by Villeroy & Boch. 2: Chef Marcello Kostenbader. (Left) Queensland tiger prawns with pawpaw, avocado and chili lime dressing; (right) Grilled fillet of beef with green corn pudding and red wine shallot glaze; (back) Caramelized pineapple pie with rum sauce. 3: This modern resort hotel opened in September 1988 at the north end of the Gold Coast, Australia's largest resort area.

PELICANS
Pan Pacific Gold Coast
81 Surf Parade, P.O.Box 174,
Broadbeach, Queensland 4218, Australia
Tel:075-92 2250 Fax:075-92 3747
Telex:AA142877
日本事務所：0

1: カジュアルな雰囲気のレストラン「ペリカンズ」は、内部に「バー」がある。エグゼクティブ・シェフはW・メイヤー。料理は左からフルーツとコッテージ・チーズ。サーロイン・ステーキのグリル。ブラック・ベリーのムース。中央奥がシーフード・プレーター。2: ゴールド・コースト南部のブロードビーチの190店舗から成る"ザ・オアシス・オン・ブロードビーチ"を代表するホテル。開業は1989年。

1: *Pelicans* has a casual ambience and includes a bar. Werner Meyer is executive chef. (From left) Fruit array with cottage cheese; grilled sirloin steak; blackberry mousse gâteau; (rear center) seafood platter (with oysters, squid, mussels, prawns, smoked salmon, crab and lobster). 2: This hotel is part of *The Oasis on Broadbeach*, a complex which includes 190 stores. It opened in 1989 at Broadbeach, at the southern end of Australia's Gold Coast.

MACROSSANS
Sheraton Mirage Port Douglas
P.O.Box 172, Port Douglas,
Queensland 4871, Australia
Tel:070-99-5888 Fax:070-98-5885
Telex:AA48888
日本事務所：T

1：オーストラリア独特の料理を提供するレストラン「マクロサンズ」。エグゼクティブ・シェフはクラウス・シェーファー。食器はヴィレロイ・アンド・ボッホ焼、デルタ・デザイン。2：地元のエビ、ホタテ、カニ爪、魚などを使ったシーフード、サフラン・ソース。3：バッファローのフィレ、アルマニャック・ソース。オーストラリア産の水牛肉、ソースはフルーツとアルマニャックを3週間煮込んだもの。4：グレート・バリア・リーフのケアンズの北方100kmにあり、2万㎡の人工プール、18ホールのゴルフ場が設けられている。開業は1987年。

●●●

1: *Macrossans* offers a number of unique Australian dishes. Klaus Schaefer is the executive chef. The servingware is Delta pattern Villeroy & Boch china. 2: Assorted local seafood (prawns, scallops, crab claw and fish) with saffron sauce. 3: Fillet of buffalo with armagnac sauce. The buffalo is Australian water buffalo, stewed for three weeks in a sauce of fruit and armagnac. 4: Located 100 kilometers north of Cairns, a port city of the Great Barrier Reef, this hotel sits in the middle of a 5.2-acre man-made pool. The hotel opened in 1987, and its facilities include an 18-hole golf course.

ORIENTAL RESTAURANT
Hayman Resort
Hayman Island,
North Queensland 4801, Australia
Tel: 079-46-9100 Fax: 079-46-9410
Telex: AA48163 Hayman
日本事務所：I

1: シェフのS.M.チャン、レストラン・マネージャーのウェンデイ・フル女史。料理は左から伊勢エビの四川風。ブドウを形どった魚のフライ。オーストラリア産マッド・クラブのソテー。2: 専用高速艇がヘイマン島までゲストを運んでくれる。超高級リゾート・ホテル。全面改装を施して1987年に再開。3: 7つあるレストランのうち、中国、日本、タイの料理が楽しめる「オリエンタル・レストラン」。

1: Chef Simon M. Chan and restaurant manager Wendy Full. (From left) Szechwan-style chili crayfish (a sweet-tasting pan-fried crayfish with chili); Shanghai-style fried fillet of fish (a traditional fish dish in the shape of a bunch of grapes, with sweet and sour sauce); sautéed Queensland mud crab (Chinese-style crab sautéed with ginger and shallots). 2: Guests are taxied to this top-class resort hotel from Hayman Island by high-speed boat. The hotel underwent a complete renovation in 1987. 3: *Oriental Restaurant* is one of seven dining facilities here. Chinese, Japanese and Thai dishes are served.

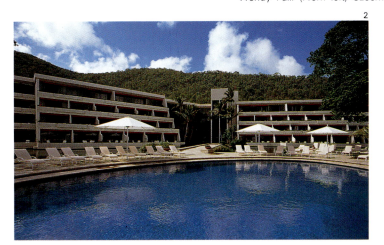

THE BRADSHAW ROOM
Sheraton Alice Springs Hotel
Barrett Drive, P.O.Box 1634
Alice Springs, N.T. 0871, Australia
Tel: 089-52 8000 Fax: 089-52 3822
日本事務所：T

1：レストラン「ザ・ブラッドショー・ルーム」は、ここでしか味わえない特別料理が自慢。2：カンガルーのステーキ。お好みによりオオボクトウの幼虫のソースをかける。オオボクトウは、木の根に寄生する幼虫で、オーストラリアの原住民が好んで食べた。焼くとバター・ピーナッツの味がする。3：ワニとカンガルーのテリーヌ、オレンジとラズベリー・ソース。4：ラクダのステーキ。5：ワニのステーキ。ちなみに、ワニは野生動物を保護するワシントン条約品目に入っているが、ここで食べさせるワニ肉はすべて養殖によるもの。6：エグゼクティブ・シェフのアマデオ．A．ザルゾッサ。7：オーストラリアの中央部アリス・スプリングスに開発されたホテル。18ホールのゴルフ場を付設して、1985年に開業。

●●●

1: *The Bradshaw Room* boasts a number of unique dishes not available anywhere else. 2: Kangaroo steak, served plain or with witchetty grub sauce. Witchetty grubs, an insect larva, have been a favorite food of the Australian aboriginal peoples; when cooked they taste something like buttered peanuts. 3: Crocodile and kangaroo terrine with orange and raspberry sauce. 4: Camel steak. 5: Crocodile steak. Since wild crocodiles are protected as an endangered species, all the crocodile meat used here is from farm-bred crocodiles. 6: Executive chef Amadeo A. Zarzosa. 7: An 18-hole golf course is among the facilities offered by this hotel, located in Alice Springs in central Australia and open since 1985.

BREEZES
Hilton International Cairns
Wharf Street, Cairns, Queensland 4870, Australia
Tel:070-52 1599 Fax:070-52 1370
日本事務所：G

1：地元シーフードとインターナショナル料理のレストラン「ブリージズ（そよ風）」。土、日曜日の夕食には"シーフード・ビュッフェ"が楽しめる。2：グレート・バリア・リーフのケアンズに1987年11月に開業。3：左からエグゼクティブ・スー・シェフのグイド・ヴァン・ベーレンとスー・シェフのパンタッキーニ・マックス。ヨーロッパ料理をアレンジしたオーストラリア料理を創作。4：「シー・ブリーズ」と名付けられた3種のソースが楽しめる魚料理。5：テーブルセッティング。

1: *Breezes* is a casual restaurant specializing in local seafood and international cuisine. On Saturday and Sunday evenings a seafood buffet is served. 2: This hotel began operation in November 1987 in the port city of Cairns, at the tip of the Great Barrier Reef. 3: Executive sous-chef Guido van Baelen (left) and sous-chef Pantacchini Max. Here Australian dishes are arranged in European style. 4: Diners can enjoy "sea breeze"—three varieties of sauce (white wine sauce, herb cream sauce and tomato sauce)—with their seafood dishes. 5: A table setting.

1
2

182 —— AUSTRALIA

KINGSFORDS
Cairns International Hotel
17 Abbott Street, Cairns,
North Queensland 4870, Australia
Tel:070-31 1300 Fax:070-31 1801
日本事務所：U

1,2："ヌーヴェル・クイジーヌ・フランセーズ"の影響を受けたレストラン「キングズフォーズ」。食器はヴィレロイ・アンド・ボッホ焼、シエナ・マーブル・デザイン。「カクテル・バー」が入口にある。3：港町ケアンズに1988年7月に開業。4：エグゼクティブ・シェフはジョン・サーグッド。80年代前半には、前オーストラリア首相マルコルム・フレーザーの料理人を勤めた。シドニーのウェントワース・ホテル、リージェント・シドニーなどを経て現職。5：仔ヒツジのフィレのサラダ、ミント・ヨーグルトのドレッシング。6：マッド・クラブのカニ爪、キノコと豪州産ブラック・ビーンの実添え。7：メレンゲとアイスクリーム、フルーツ添え。イチゴとパパイヤのソース。チョコレート・ヴァニラ・ソースが美しくデザインされたデザート。

●●●

1, 2: *Kingsfords* restaurant includes a *Cocktail Bar* near the entrance. The food is heavily influenced by Nouvelle Cuisine Française. The servingware is Villeroy & Boch china in a Sienna marble pattern. **3:** This Cairns hotel opened in July 1988. **4:** Executive chef John Thurgood cooked for former Australian Prime Minister Malcolm Fraser in the early 1980's. He also worked at Sydney's Wentworth Hotel and the Regent Sydney. **5:** Salad of marinated lamb fillet with mint yogurt dressing. **6:** Poached mud crab with trumpet and oyster mushrooms, served with black bean and lime bouillon. **7:** A beautifully prepared dessert consisting of a meringue basket with cassis ice cream and macerated tropical fruits, served with strawberry papaya sauce and chocolate vanilla sauce.

PETRIES
Hyatt Regency Coolum
P.O.Box 78, Coolum,
Queensland 4573, Australia
Tel:61-71-462-777 Fax:61-71-462-957
Telex:70963
日本事務所：E

1: レストラン「ペトリーズ」は、"スパ・クイジーン"と名付けられた低カロリー料理も提供する。2: 左からレストラン・マネージャーのギャリー・フレンド。ドイツ生れのシェフのジョゼフ・イーダー。食器はヴィレロイ・アンド・ボッホ焼、カレイドスコープ・デザイン。3: オーストラリア最初のヘルス・スパ付設のオール・スイートのゴルフ・リゾート・ホテル。開業は1988年6月。

1: *Petries* restaurant offers a low-calorie, healthy menu of "spa cuisine." 2: Restaurant manager Garry Friend (left) and German-born chef Josef Eder. The china is Kaleidoscope pattern by Villeroy & Boch. 3: This golf resort hotel also includes Australia's first complete health spa facilities. The all-suite hotel started operation in June 1988.

FLINDERS
Sheraton Darwin Hotel
32 Mitchell Street, Darwin, N.T. 0800, Australia
Tel: 089-82 0000 Fax: 089-81 1765
日本事務所：T

1：ロビーを見渡す3階にあるレストラン「フリンダーズ」。18世紀イギリスの海洋探検家・水路測量技師マテュー・フリンダーズ（1774〜1814）にちなんでいる。入口に「フリンダーズ・ラウンジ」。2：ポート・ダーウィンに1986年7月開業した近代ホテル。3：左から給仕長のホセ・ラモス。シニアー・スー・シェフのクリスチャン・モンターニュ。シーフードを主体としたレストランで、夜7時から営業。

1: *Flinders* restaurant is on the third floor and looks out on the lobby. *Flinders Lounge* is near the restaurant entrance. Both take their name from Matthew Flinders (1774–1814), an English seafaring explorer and nautical surveyor. 2: This modern hotel serves the city of Darwin in northern Australia. It opened in July 1986. 3: From left: maître d'hôtel Jose Ramos and senior sous-chef Christian Montagne. The restaurant specializes in seafood and is open every evening from 7 p.m.

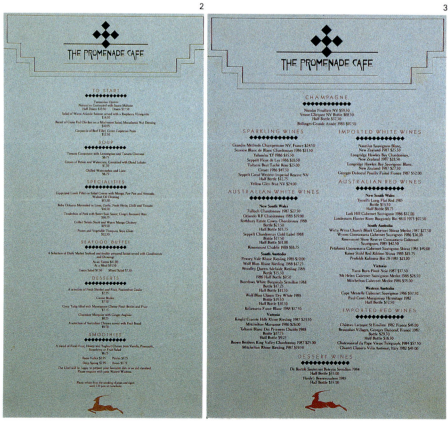

4

THE PROMENADE CAFÉ
The Hyatt Hotel Canberra
Overlooking Lake Burley Griffin,
Commonwealth Ave,
Yarralumta A.C.T. 2600, Australia
Tel:062-70-1234 Fax:062-81-5998
Telex: AA61326
日本事務所：E

1,7：旧館と新館をつなぐ廊下の両脇にあるレストラン「ザ・プロムナード・カフェ」。エグゼクティブ・シェフはスティーヴン・リウ。香港とヨーロッパのホテルで修業。1984年、フランクフルトのフード・オリンピックでゴールド・メダルを獲得。2,3：メニューとワイン・リスト。4：1924年に開業した首都キャンベラのホテル。1988年に増築して再開業。5：大西洋産サーモンのグリル、ラズベリー・ビネガー・ソース。6：マカデミア・ナッツ入り鶏の胸肉、白ワイン・ソース、ワイルド・ライスと野菜添え。ソースはドイツ産白ワインを使っている。

●●●

1, 7: *The Promenade Café* occupies both sides of the passageway connecting the original building with the new wing. Executive chef Steven P.C. Liu trained in Hong Kong and Europe, and in 1984 won a gold medal in a contest at the Frankfurt Food Olympics. 2, 3: The menu and wine list. 4: This hotel began business in 1924 in the Australian capital of Canberra. After extensive renovation and expansion it reopened in 1988. 5: A warm salad of grilled Atlantic salmon served with raspberry vinaigrette. 6: Breast of chicken stuffed with macadamia nuts and served with wild rice and Riesling white wine sauce.

5

6

7

Great Hotels of the World: vol. 5 — 187

ホテル日本事務所 リスト

A.
ホテル オークラ チェーン
105 東京都港区虎ノ門2-10-4　ホテルオークラ内
Tel:(03)3582-0111　Fax:(03)3589-4446
フリーダイヤル:0120-003741

D.
ホリデイ・インズ・インターナショナル・
リザベーション・オフィス
150 東京都渋谷区渋谷2-6-4　ライベスト青山6階
Tel:(03)5485-0311　Fax:(03)5485-0331
フリーダイヤル:0120-381489(大阪06地域のみ)

B.
コンコルド ホテルズ
104 東京都中央区築地4-1-1　東劇ビル6F
Tel:(03)3545-9571　Fax:(03)3545-9573

E.
ハイアット・ホテルズ・アンド・リゾーツ
102 東京都千代田区麹町5-3　第7秋山ビル7F
Tel:(03)3222-0441 予約(03)3222-0391
　　(06)764-6144
Fax:(03)3222-0390

C.
フォー・シーズンズ・ホテルズ・アンド・リゾーツ
102 東京都千代田区平河町2-1-2
　　住友半蔵門ビル別館5階
Tel:(03)3288-9511　Fax:(03)3288-9510

F.
ヒルトン・ホテルズ・コーポレーション
100 東京都千代田区有楽町1-8-1
　　日比谷パークビル315号室
Tel:(03)3213-4051、4056
Fax:(03)3214-0647

G.
ヒルトン・インターナショナル
102 東京都千代田区麹町5-7
　　秀和紀尾井町TBR915
Tel: (03)3262-8981　Fax: (03)3262-8970

K.
マリオットホテル・リゾート&スイート日本支社
100 東京都千代田区丸の内3-1-1
国際ビルB159号
Tel: (03)3215-7258　Fax: (03)3215-7290
フリーダイヤル(東京23区以外):0120-142536

N.
ニッコー ホテルズ インターナショナル
104 東京都中央区八重洲2-4-1
　　常和八重洲ビル9階
Tel: (03)3281-4321　Fax: (03)3284-2848

H.
インターコンチネンタルホテルズ ジャパン㈱
106 東京都港区東麻布1-7-3　第2渡辺ビル7階
Tel: (03)5561-0701　Fax: (03)5561-0722
フリーダイヤル:0120-455655

L.
マンダリン オリエンタル・ホテル グループ
105 東京都港区新橋6-5-5　アタゴ小林ビル3F
Tel: (03)3433-3388　Fax: (03)3433-3347

O.
パン・パシフィック・ホテルズ・アンド・リゾーツ
100 東京都千代田区丸の内3-1-1　新東京ビル139
Tel: (03)3214-3001　Fax: (03)3211-8002
フリーダイヤル0120-001800

I.
ザ・リーディングホテルズ・オブ・ザ・ワールド
日本支社
150 東京都渋谷区渋谷2-17-3
Tel: (03)3797-3631　Fax: (03)3797-6701

M.
ホテル・メリディアン・チェーン
107 東京都港区南青山1-1-1
新青山ビル西館15階
Tel: (03)3475-2364　Fax: (03)3475-2375

P.
ザ ペニンシュラ グループ
100 東京都千代田区有楽町1-5-2
東宝ツインタワービル6階
Tel: (03)3595-8084　Fax: (03)3502-2467

J.
ルレー・エ・シャトー
150 東京都渋谷区神宮前6-12-5
Tel: (03)3407-8889　Fax: (03)3407-8055

Q.
ラマダ・インターナショナル日本セールス オフィス
102 東京都千代田区一番町22-1
　一番町セントラルビル601号室
Tel:(03)3239-8303　Fax:(03)3239-6986

T.
シェラトン・ホテルズ
102 東京都千代田区紀尾井町4-1
ホテル・ニューオータニ内
Tel:(03)3264-4751　Fax:(03)3264-0791
フリーダイヤル:0120-003535

W.
タージ・インターナショナル・ホテルズ
108 東京都港区三田3-14-11　鳥和三田ビル6F
Tel:(03)3453-3393　Fax:(03)3453-3780

R.
リージェント・インターナショナル・ホテル日本支社
100 東京都千代田区有楽町1-10-1
　有楽町ビル70号室
Tel:(03)3211-4541　Fax:(03)3211-4538

U.
㈱大京　海外事業部
151 東京都渋谷区千駄ヶ谷4-24-13
Tel:(03)3475-3812　Fax:(03)3423-0487

X.
ユーテル インターナショナル
105 東京都港区浜松町2-2-5　浜松町営和ビル5階
Tel:(03)3435-9311　Fax:(03)3435-9319

S.
シャングリラ インターナショナル日本支社
103 東京都中央区日本橋小網町14-1
　日新ビル6階
Tel:(03)3667-7744　Fax:(03)3667-7743

V.
シンガポール・マンダリン・インターナショナルホテルズ
日本支社
105 東京都港区新橋5-5-1　イーグルビル5階
Tel:(03)3432-4462　Fax:(03)3432-4531

Y.
ウエスティン・ホテル・アンド・リゾート
100 東京都千代田区有楽町1-8-1
日比谷パークビル403号室
Tel:(03)3213-1671(個人)、
　　(03)3213-1674(グループ)
　　(03)3214-1830(セールス)
Fax:(03)3213-4558
フリーダイヤル(東京23区以外)0120-391671

Profile

岸川惠俊

1951年、北海道小樽市に生まれる。1972年より、ワールド・カップ・スキー・レース、国際自動車ラリーの記録映画、TV番組などのムービー・カメラマンとして世界を廻る。1982年より、フォト・ジャーナリストに転向。以来、ライフワークとして、世界のホテル取材を開始する。年6ヵ月を海外取材に費し、1990年11月現在までに、世界の一流ホテル200ヵ所の取材を終える。日本商工会議所「石垣」(87-90)、柴田書店「ホテル・旅館」、プレジデント・クラブ「ステイタス」などの月刊誌に連載ページをもつ。企業ポスター、カレンダーなどの広告メディアにも、多くの写真を提供。1987年度、日野自動車カレンダー・世界の窓シリーズで全国カレンダー展入賞。

Hiro Kishikawa

Hiro Kishikawa was born in 1951 on Japan's northernmost island of Hokkaido. In 1972 he began working as a cameraman, traveling around the world covering World Cup ski races, international auto rallies and similar events. In 1982 he switched to photography, specializing in international hotels, and by November 1990, after traveling six months of each year, he had completed photo studies of some 200 first-class hotels around the world. He is a regular contributor to several monthly trade magazines in Japan, and has also provided many photographs for posters, calendars and other advertising media, including a 1987 calendar that won a prize in a Japanese nationwide calendar competition.

桐敷真次郎

1926年、東京都生まれ。1950年、東京大学工学部建築学科卒業。同大学院、ロンドン大学コートオールド美術研究所研究生を経て、1959年、一級建築士。1960年、東京都立大学工学部建築工学科助教授。1962年、工学博士。1971年、東京都立大学教授。1990年、東京家政学院大学教授。『建築学大系5・西洋建築史』『明治の建築』『建築史』『パラーディオ「建築四書」注解』等、著書・論文多数。1987年度日本建築学会賞(論文賞)受賞。第10回マルコ・ポーロ賞受賞。

Shinjiro Kirishiki

Born in Tokyo in 1926, Shinjiro Kirishiki graduated from Department of Architecture, University of Tokyo in 1950. After studying as a graduate student of University of Tokyo and as a research student of University of London, he was registered architect in 1959 and was appointed Associate Professor of Architectural History, Department of Architecture, Tokyo Metropolitan University in 1960. In 1962 he was conferred D.Eng. from University of Tokyo. Since 1971, he was Professor of Architectural History and Design of the same university and an active member of the Architectural Institute of Japan. Professor Kirishiki is the author of "Architectural History," "Architecture of Meiji Period," "Commentary on Palladio's Four Books of Architecture," and many other books, papers and articles. He was awarded the 1986 Thesis Prize of the Architectural Institute of Japan and also the 10th Marco Polo Prize from the Istituto Italiano di Cultura in 1987. In 1990, he became Professor Emeritus of Tokyo Metropolitan University and Professor of Tokyo Kasei Gakuin University.

GREAT HOTELS OF THE WORLD: VOL.5
HOTEL RESTAURANT

初版印刷	1992年4月20日
初版発行	1992年4月30日
写真・文	岸川惠俊
監修	桐敷真次郎
デザイン	北澤敏彦＋株式会社ディス・ハウス
翻訳	ロブ・サターホワイト
発行者	清水 勝
発行所	河出書房新社
	〒151 東京都渋谷区千駄ヶ谷2-32-2
	電話:(営業)03-3404-1201/(編集)03-3404-8611
	振替:東京0-10802
印刷	大日本印刷株式会社
製本	大口製本印刷株式会社

Copyright © Kawade Shobo Shinsha Publishers Ltd, 1992
Photography & Text copyright © Hiro Kishikawa, 1992

本書からの二次使用(転載)は、著作権者の許可を必要とします。
また、コンピューター・ソフトへの写真入力使用、写真のトリミング使用、
写真の機械・電子的使用、フォトコピー、本書の録音など、
本書からの無断使用を禁じます。

落丁本、乱丁本はお取り替えします。
定価は帯・カバーに表示してあります。

ISBN4-309-71585-0